More Sussex

Walks

Originally compiled by
John Brooks

Fully revised by David Foster,
Nick Channer and David Hancock

Text: John Brooks
                      Revised text for 2006 edition,
                      David Foster and Nick Channer
                      Revised text 2009, David Hancock
Photography: John Brooks, Nick Channer
Editorial: Ark Creative (UK) Ltd
Design: Ark Creative (UK) Ltd

 This product includes mapping data licensed from
Ordnance Survey® with the permission of the Controller
of Her Majesty's Stationery Office. © Crown Copyright
2009. All rights reserved. Licence number 150002047. Ordnance Survey, the
OS symbol and Pathfinder are registered trademarks and Explorer,
Landranger and Outdoor Leisure are trademarks of the Ordnance Survey, the
national mapping agency of Great Britain.

ISBN   978-0-7117-2083-1

While every care has been taken to ensure the accuracy of the route
directions, the publishers cannot accept responsibility for errors or
omissions, or for changes in details given. The countryside is not static:
hedges and fences can be removed, field boundaries can alter, footpaths
can be rerouted and changes in ownership can result in the closure or
diversion of some concessionary paths. Also, paths that are easy and
pleasant for walking in fine conditions may become slippery, muddy and
difficult in wet weather, while stepping stones across rivers and streams
may become impassable.

If you find an inaccuracy in either the text or maps, please write to
Crimson Publishing at the address below.

First published 2002 by Jarrold Publishing
Revised and reprinted 2006, 2008, 2009.

This edition first published in Great Britain 2008 by Crimson Publishing,
a division of:
Crimson Business Ltd,
Westminster House, Kew Road, Richmond, Surrey, TW9 2ND
www.totalwalking.co.uk

Printed in Singapore. 3/09

A catalogue record for this book is available from the British library.

Front cover: The view from above Bopeep Chalk Pit
Previous page: Bewl Water

Contents

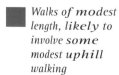

Short, easy walks

Walks of modest
length, likely to
involve some
modest uphill
walking

More challenging
walks which may
be longer and/or
over more rugged
terrain, often with
some stiff climbs

Contents

Keymap 1

Bentley
Shackleford
Waverley Abbey
Peper Harow
Eashing
Bramley
GODALMING
Shamley Green
Rowledge
Millbridge
Tilford
Elstead
Milford
Busbridge
Thorncombe Street
Bucks Horn Oak
Blacknest
Spreakley
Frensham
Wheelerstreet
Hydestile
Rowly
Wheatley
Batt's Corner
Rushmoor
Thursley
Witley
Hascombe
Kingsley
Churt
Bowlhead Green
Brook
Hambledon
Sleaford
Lindford
Arford
Headley Down
Wormley
Loxhill
Dunsfold
Bordon Camp
Hindhead
Gibbet Hill
Chiddingfold
Alfold
Whitehill
Headley
Standford
Grayshott
Grayswood
BORDON
Shottermill
HASLEMERE
Ramsnest Common
Conford
Bramshott
Longmoor Camp
Liphook
Camelsdale
Fisherstreet
Ifold
Linchmere
Kingsley Green
Plaistow
Greatham
Liss Forest
Langley
LOW
East Liss
Fernhurst
Northchapel
Rake
Milland
Lurgashall
Kirdford
Henley
Lickfold
Balls Cross
Wisborough Green
Terwick Common
Rother
Chithurst
Iping
Woolbeding
Easebourne
Lodsworth
Rogate
Trotton
Stedham
Upperton
Petworth House
Petworth
MIDHURST
Nyewood
Tillington
Nursted
East Harting
West Lavington
Selham
R Rother
Byworth
Fittleworth
Elsted
South Ambersham
Didling
South Harting
Coultershaw Bridge
Stopham
Treyford
ROMAN ROAD
Bepton
Heyshott
Hardham
Uppark
Cocking
Graffham
East Lavington
Duncton
Coldwaltham
Wiggonholt
North Marden
South Downs Way
SOUTH DOWNS
Barlavington
Greatham
Chilgrove
Sutton
ROMAN VILLA
Waterfield
Compton
Bignor
Rackham
East Marden
Singleton
Upwaltham
West Burton
Bury
Charlton
East Dean
Castle
Amberley
West Dean
Houghton
Stoughton
STANE STREET
North Stoke
The Trundle
Madehurst
Walderton
Arundel Park
South Stoke
Woodend
West Stoke
Lavant
Goodwood House
Eartham
Slindon
Burpham
Funtington
Halnaker
Woodmancote
East Ashling
Fontwell
Warningcamp
Boxgrove
West Ashling
Strettington
Castle
ARUNDEL
Hambrook
ROMAN PALACE
Westhampnett
Norton
Walberton
Nutbourne
Tangmere
Nyton
Crossbush
Hermitage
Aldingbourne
Tortington
SWORTH
Southbourne
Broadbridge
Westergate
Eastergate
Barnham
Lyminster
Thorney Island
Fishbourne
CHICHESTER
Toddington
Bosham
Woodgate
Ford
Merston
Colworth
Apuldram
Shripney
Yapton
West Thorney
Donnington
Bosham Hoe
Runcton
Flansham
Climping
Rustington
North Mundham
Hunston
West Itchenor
Chichester Harbour
Bersted
Ancton
Birdham
South Mundham
LITTLEHA
Shipton Green
Hayling
Street End
Felpham
Middleton-on-Sea
Nyetimber
BOGNOR REGIS
Somerley
Aldwick
West Wittering
Sidlesham
Highleigh
Pagham
Pagham Harbour
East Wittering
Earnley
Bracklesham Bay
Church Norton
Selsey
SELSEY BILL
A3
A325
A287
A286
A283
A281
A272
A27
A259
A29
A285
A284
B3001
B3002
B3004
B2131
B2130
B2128
B2133
B2070
B2146
B2141
B2147
B2178
B2179
B2198
B2145
B2166
B2233
B2138
1
3
8
17
18
21
22
25
28

Paddock Wood · Claygate · Marden · Staplehurst · Pluckley Thor · Pluckley Sta
B2160 · B2079 · Marden Thorn · Smarden · Maltman's Hill
Brenchley · Winchet Hill · Curtisden Green · Frittenden · Haffenden Quarter · Bethi
Kipping's Cross · Horsmonden · A229 · Standen · Curteis Corner
Lamberhurst · Goudhurst · A262 · Iden Green · Sissinghurst · Three Chimneys · Biddenden · High Halden · ROMAN ROAD
Scotney Castle · Kilndown · Gill's Green · Cranbrook Common · A262 · Shirkoak
The Down · Hartley · Cranbrook · East End · 276 · TENTERDEN · St Michaels · B2067 · Woodchurc
Vadhurst · Bedgebury Forest · Benenden · Hole Park · Leigh Green · Shirley
Three Leg Cross · Flimwell · Gill's Green · Iden Green · B2086 · Rolvenden · Small Hythe · Reading Street
Ticehurst · A268 · High Street · Hawkhurst · Four Throws · A28 · Rolvenden Layne · B2082 · B206
Stonegate · The Moor · A268 · Sandhurst · Linkhill · Newenden · I S L E · O F · Wittersham · The Stocks · Stone in O
Witherenden Hill · A265 · Hurst Green · Silver Hill · Bodiam · Castle · Great Dixter · Northiam · Rother · Four Oaks · Iden · A268
Burwash · Etchingham · Salehurst · Ewhurst Green · B2088 · Beckley · Peasmarsh · Playden
Batemans · Robertsbridge · Mill Corner · B2165 · Rye Foreign · RYE
Oxley's Green · A21 · Staplecross · Cripp's Corner · B2089 · Broad Oak · Broadland Row · Udimore · B2089 · Camber Castle
Darwell Resr · John's Cross · Vinehall Street · Sedlescombe · Brede · River Brede · Winchelsea · Winchelsea B
Brightling · Mountfield · Netherfield · Whatlington · Icklesham · Westfield · A259
Dallington · Penhurst · BATTLE · Abbey · Beauport Park · Telham · Guestling Green · Pett · Cliff End
Ashburnham Place · Catsfield · B2095 · Baldslow · Crowhurst · A21 · B2093 · Fairlight · Fairlight Cove
Windmill Hill · Ninfield · Henley's Down · Lower Street · Hollington · Ore
Boreham Street · Hooe Common · Lunsford's Cross · A269 · Castle · HASTINGS
Wartling · Hooe · Sidley · Bulverhythe · St Leonards
A259 · Little Common · BEXHILL
Pevensey Bay · Norman's Bay Station
Pevensey Bay · Langney Point · URNE

Royal Sovereign

SCALE 1:250 000 or 1 INCH to 4 MILES *1CM to 2.5KM*
0 — 2 — 4 — 6 — 8 — 10 — KILOMETRES — 15
0 — 2 — 4 — 6 — MILES — 8 — 10
KEYMAP HEIGHTS SHOWN IN METRES

Walk	Page	Start	Nat. Grid Reference	Distance	Time	Highest Point
Airman's Grave and Duddleswell	22	Fairwarp church	TQ 465267	3½ miles (5.5km)	2 hrs	541ft (165m)
Ardingly Reservoir	26	Ardingly Reservoir car park	TQ 334287	5 miles (8km)	2½ hrs	426ft (130m)
Battle – 1066 Country Walk	16	Battle Abbey gate	TQ 748158	3½ miles (5.6km)	2 hrs	183ft (56m)
Beachy Head and Long Down	58	Old Lighthouse, west of Beachy Head	TV 566954	6½ miles (10.5km)	3 hrs	538ft (164m)
Belloc's Mill	38	School Lane, Shipley	TQ 143219	6 miles (9.7km)	3 hrs	98ft (30m)
Bewl Water from Wadhurst	30	Wadhurst	TQ 641317	5½ miles (8.9km)	2½ hrs	447ft (136m)
Bignor Hill and the River Arun	86	Summit of Bignor Hill	SU 973129	11 miles (17.7km)	5 hrs	731ft (223m)
Blackcap and Stanmer Down from Ditchling	71	Ditchling Beacon	TQ 333129	8½ miles (13.7km)	4 hrs	771ft (235m)
Bosham and Fishbourne from West Itchenor	77	West Itchenor	SU 798012	9½ miles (15.3km)	5 hrs	27ft (8m)
Burwash and Bateman's	74	Burwash	TQ 672246	7½ miles (12.1km)	3 hrs	519ft (158m)
Chidham Peninsula	28	Chidham	SU 793034	5 miles (8km)	2½ hrs	16ft (5m)
Cissbury Ring	20	Findon	TQ 139085	4 miles (6.4km)	1½ hrs	604ft (184m)
Cuckmere Haven from Seaford	24	Seaford seafront	TV 484984	5 miles (8km)	2½ hrs	227ft (69m)
Cuckmere River and Norton Top from Alfriston	80	Alfriston	TQ 521032	9 miles (14.5km)	4-4½ hrs	391ft (119m)
Downland Hills from Devil's Dyke	61	Devil's Dyke inn	TQ 258110	8 miles (12.9km)	3½ hrs	689ft (210m)
Downland Walk from Telscombe	83	Telscombe, south of Lewes	TQ 404032	11 miles (17.7km)	5 hrs	417ft (127m)
Durford Heath and Rogate Common	14	National Trust car park, Durford Heath	SU 790259	3½ miles (5.6km)	2 hrs	475ft (145m)
Hastings Country Park	50	Visitor Centre, Fairlight	TQ 860116	6 miles (9.7km)	3 hrs	466ft (142m)
Herstmonceux	35	Herstmonceux	TQ 634125	5½ miles (8.9km)	3 hrs	164ft (50m)
Icklesham from Winchelsea	47	Winchelsea	TQ 905173	6½ miles (10.5km)	3 hrs	178ft (54m)
Kingley Vale, Stoughton and Walderton	67	West Stoke, car park	SU 824088	8½ miles (13.7km)	4½ hrs	672ft (205m)
Lodsworth and Lickfold from Cowdray Park	64	Benbow Pond, Cowdray Park	SU 914222	8 miles (12.9km)	4 hrs	442ft (135m)
Rye from Iden	44	Iden church	TQ 914237	6 miles (9.7km)	3 hrs	151ft (46m)
Temple of the Winds from Fernhurst	52	Fernhurst	SU 896284	6 miles (9.7km)	3 hrs	902ft (275m)
Three Commons Walk	18	Iping Common car park	SU 852219	4 miles (6.4km)	2 hrs	119ft (36m)
Wey and Arun Canal from Billingshurst	41	Billingshurst library	TQ 086260	6 miles (9.7km)	3 hrs	114ft (35m)
Wolstonbury from Hurstpierpoint	32	Hurstpierpoint	TQ 281165	5½ miles (8.9km)	3 hrs	675ft (206m)
Woolbeding Common and Hammer Wood	55	Woolbeding Common	SU 869260	7 miles (11.3km)	4 hrs	600ft (183m)

CRAWLEY • HORLEY • Smallfield • London (Gatwick) Airport • Copthorne • Crawley Down • Crabbet Park • Turners Hill • Worth • Worth Abbey • Three Bridges • Ifield • Broadfield • Pease Pottage • Colgate • ST LEONARD'S FOREST • Handcross • Balcombe • Staplefield • Slaugham • Warninglid • Brook Street • Whitemans Green • CUCKFIELD • Ansty • Bolney • Wivelsfield Sta • BURGESS HILL • Hurstpierpoint • Hassocks • Keymer • Clayton • Ditchling • Ditchling Beacon • Pyecombe • Patcham • Stanmer • Moulsecoomb • Bevendean • Coldean • BRIGHTON • HOVE • Kemp Town • Rottingdean

HORSHAM • Warnham • Broadbridge Heath • Roffey • Slinfold • Itchingfield • Mannings Heath • Christ's Hospital • Barns Green • Five Oaks • Southwater • Nuthurst • Lower Beeding • Crabtree • Copsale • Maplehurst • Cowfold • Monastery • Wineham • Hickstead • Twineham • Sayers Common • Albourne

BILLINGSHURST • Coneyhurst • Brooks Green • Dragons Green • Shipley • Littleworth • West Grinstead • Dial Post • Coolham • Broadford Bridge • Gay Street • Nutbourne • West Chiltington • Ashurst • Henfield • Blackstone • Partridge Green • Small Dole • Edburton • Woodmancote • Thakeham • Ablingworth • Ashington • Wiston • Storrington • Washington • Sullington • Steyning • Bramber • Upper Beeding • Poynings • Fulking • Devil's Dyke

Kithurst Hill • South Downs Way • Harrow Hill • North End • Findon • Cissbury Ring • Patching • Clapham • High Salvington • Upper Cokeham • Sompting • Lancing • Shoreham Airport • Shoreham-by-Sea • Shoreham Beach • Kingston by Sea • SOUTHWICK • PORTSLADE-BY-SEA • North Lancing • South Lancing • Botolphs • Coombes • Mile Oak • Portslade

ANGMERING • Durrington • Broadwater • WORTHING • Goring-by-Sea • Ferring • East Preston • Kingston Gorse

Cranleigh • Rudgwick • Bucks Green • Ellen's Green • Oakwoodhill • Capel • Ockley • Kingsfold • Rowhook • Faygate • Newdigate • Charlwood • Parkgate • Beare Green • Holmwood • Anstiebury • Coldharbour • Leith Hill • Hurt Wood • Peaslake • Holmbury St Mary

Markers: 13, 12, 7, 10, 23, 20, 4, 5

Roads: A24, A264, A23, A272, A281, A283, A280, A27, A259, A2037, A2300, A281, B2110, B2115, B2116, B2117, B2118, B2126, B2127, B2128, B2133, B2135, A29, B2036, B2037, B2038, B2112

Lingfield
Marsh Green
Hever
Castle
Penshurst Place
Bidborough
Crockhurst Street
Cap

A22
Dormansland
Dormans Park
565
Cowden
Markbeech
Cowden Sta.
Penshurst
B2176
Southborough
A26
Pembu

A264
Felcourt
Blackham
Ashurst
Fordcombe
Speldhurst
A21

EAST GRINSTEAD
Ashurst Wood
A264
ROMAN ROAD
B2026
Langton Green
ROYAL TUNBRIDGE WELLS
A264
A26

Felbridge
489
Forest Row
Hartfield
Groombridge
A26
Bells Yew Green
B2169

Sunnyside Saint Hill
B2110
Upper Hartfield
Withyham
Eridge Green
Frant
Durgates

Selsfield Common
Weir Wood
Coleman's Hatch
Frier's Gate
Eridge Sta.
B2100

Sharpthorne
HIGH
ASHDOWN FOREST
715
788
Boarshead
Steel Cross
Mark Cross
Best Beech Hill

Wych Cross
666
Nutley
3
CROWBOROUGH
Town Row
Greenhill
Tidebrook

Highbrook
Chelwood Gate
Jarvis Brook
B2100
Rotherfield
646
Argos' Hill
Coggins Mill

Ardingly
Horsted Keynes
Danehill
Fairwarp
High Hurstwood
Butchers Cross
River Rother

HAYWARDS HEATH
Scayne's Hill
Sheffield Park Sta.
Fletching
Maresfield
A272
Hadlow Down
Five Ashes
Mayfield

Newick
A272
Buxted
Ringles Cross
B2102
Cross in Hand
Broad Oak
A265

Wivelsfield
11
UCKFIELD
New Town
256
Blackboys
Possingworth Park
HEATHFIELD
Clade Street
Punn

Wivelsfield Green
Chailey
Ridgewood
Framfield
B2192
Waldron
Little London
Chapel Cross

LOW WEALD
South Street
Spithurst
Isfield
Little Horsted
A22
Halland
Foxhunt Green
Horam
Maynard's Green
Warbleton
Fool

Plumpton Green
East Chiltington
Barcombe Cross
Shortgate
Whitesmith
East Hoathly
Burlow
Vines Cross
Mile

Plumpton
Barcombe
A26
Broyle Side
Ringmer
B2124
Chiddingly
Muddles Green
Lealands
Golden Cross
Cowbeech
Stunts Green
Hellingly

Cooksbridge
Hamsey
Offham
South Malling
B2192
Cliffe Hill
639
1264
Glyndebourne
Laughton
Lower Dicker
Golden Cross
Horsebridge
11

BRIGHTON
Falmer
Kingston near Lewes
LEWES
Mount Caburn
Glynde
Ripe
Upper Dicker
Priory
HAILSHAM
Magham Down
Castle

Moulsecoomb
Bevendean
A27
Iford
Rodmell
Beddingham
13
West Firle
Selmeston
Arlington Resr.
Arlington
A22
B2104
PEVEN
LEVE

Woodingdean
B2123
Oyingdean
Southease
Tarring Neville
Firle Beacon
713
Alciston
Berwick
Wilmington
Folkington
702
Wannock
Stone Cross
Friday Street

Saltdean
Telscombe
Piddinghoe
South Heighton
Denton
Alfriston
Litlington
The Long Man
Jevington
Willingdon
Hampden Park
A22

Rottingdean
Peacehaven
A259
Rookery Hill
Bishopstone
East Blatchington
26
Westdean
East Dean
659
Willingdon Hill
A2021

NEWHAVEN
SEAFORD
6
Friston
Seaford
534
EAST

South Downs Way
Birling Gap
19
BEACHY HEAD

5   27   26   19   11   6

Comments

This wealden walk illustrates two aspects of Ashdown Forest: the sandy heathland for the outward part and varied woodland for the return. It also visits the scene of a 1941 air crash.

Part of the reservoir is used for watersports and may be noisy in summer, but the route leads away from this area to more peaceful countryside, crossing a wonderful footbridge by a nature reserve.

Most people visit Battle to view the battlefield from the Abbey grounds. Fighting also took place on the land covered by part of this short walk, which uses paths through fields and woodland.

The South Downs Way has many stretches of exhilarating walking, but nowhere is it more spectacular than here. The outward route uses field paths and tracks to cross Long Down.

Hilaire Belloc lived at Shipley and wrote eloquently about the scenery of Sussex. The walk passes through countryside that he knew and loved and uses field paths and tracks.

The walk follows the southern (Sussex) shore of the reservoir, the largest expanse of open water in southern England. Part of the route is underwalked and may be encroached by brambles and nettles.

This varied walk offers downland, riverside and woodland routes; both the longer options include a choice of pubs.

This downland walk needs careful wayfaring as part of the route lacks signposts and the paths are sometimes vague. Much of the going is on springy turf while field paths and farm tracks are also used.

Make sure that the ferry is operating when you start this walk at West Itchenor. There are no gradients on this coastal walk but it is possible to get wet boots at Bosham if the tide is exceptionally high.

Several short climbs on this undulating walk to the south of Burwash. Secluded meadows and dense woodland in places. Bateman's is well worth a look so allow longer if you are planning a visit.

Avoid this walk at high tide as part of the route is along the tideline. Birdwatchers will enjoy seeing migrants and native waders on the vast, seemingly infinite, mudbanks of Chichester harbour.

The outward route passes below the ramparts of the famous prehistoric fort. The return means climbing to the ring itself, where the reward is a magnificent view over Worthing and the coast.

Seaford was once fashionable as a resort but its grand hotels went long ago. Its shore is still attractive as is the path that climbs steeply to Seaford Head, a magnificent viewpoint for the Seven Sisters.

The walk starts from Alfriston and climbs from the river to the top of the Downs above Seaford. The return descends the north-facing slope to visit Alciston and Berwick, where there are village inns.

This may be a walk to avoid if there is a strong westerly wind. But at least you will be blown home. The outward route follows the crest of the downs while the return is on less-frequented bridleways.

Many delightful villages are hidden in the downs, but none is more attractive than Telscombe. The route stays on the top of the downs for its entire distance so be sure to take food and drink.

Much of the sandy soil of the heath is covered with woodland but you emerge into open country before returning via Rogate Common.

The outward route covers farmland, heath and woodland before emerging on East Hill overlooking Hastings Old Town. The gradients come steep and often on the return along the clifftop path.

The footpath from the village to the castle gives views over the Pevensey Levels and also allows a glimpse of Herstmonceux Place, an 18th-century house built with bricks made for the Tudor castle.

Winchelsea, perched on its hilltop, is a unique town with a violent history. Its prosperity ended when the sea retreated. The walk explores the contrasting countryside to the west, notable for its orchards.

The ancient, twisted branches of the yew trees in Kingley Vale give the place a sinister atmosphere, but the walk is far from gloomy. It covers glorious countryside and two appealing villages.

Although Lickfold is only a hamlet, Lodsworth is more substantial, with a church and pub. The route takes in a variety of landscapes but the going can be muddy.

Not only is this a scenically rewarding walk that gives superb views of Rye, but there are also advantages in not having to take a car into the town where parking is difficult at peak times.

This walk demands navigational skills and energy, with a climb of about 650ft (200m) from the start to the summit of Black Down. The way down is even steeper, and streams often run down the paths.

Good walking on sandy paths takes in Trotton and Stedham Commons, and the route also follows the Rother for a short way.

Once across the new bypass at Billingshurst, the route enters lovely countryside where you are unlikely to meet other walkers. The stretches by the canal and river offer opportunities to see kingfishers.

Field paths predominate in this excursion, and good breath is needed to climb Wolstonbury, the site of a prehistoric hillfort. There is a good view of Danny, a Tudor mansion, on the return.

Blending airy heath with shady forest, this is another Wealden route that demands wayfaring skills and where mud may be a problem. *Note the warning in the introduction to the walk.*

Introduction to Sussex

Artists who produced railway posters in the 1930s were fond of showing a hiking couple striding along a crest of the Sussex downs, the man smoking a pipe and swinging a hefty stick, the lady carrying map and haversack. They tread on springy turf below a blue sky, and you can almost hear a choir of skylarks singing overhead.

The face of the county

The face of Sussex has changed greatly in the 70 years since the posters, but the image created by the railway artist survives in the minds of walkers. Those who explore the South Downs Way will know of favoured stretches where there is still a carpet of turf underfoot, skylarks sing and butterflies rise, heavy with nectar, from wayside flowers. Yet even the most ardent Sussex supporter has to admit that there are also less attractive sections where sheep pastures have been ploughed up and sown with cereals or rape seed. Here the going may be along a hedgeless, flinty track or, even worse, on a concrete farm road running between vast fields and laid as straight as though it had been made by the Romans. Fortunately, there remains much more to satisfy than dismay, and it is only older walkers who will remember the downs before the 1970s, when the modern pattern of agriculture began in the county.

It is still the downland that attracts most walkers to Sussex even though it is an area that covers only a small proportion of the county. It extends eastwards as a wedge, its broadest point at the border with Hampshire, for about 55 miles (89km) before its spectacular meeting with the sea at Beachy Head. However, the highest point in Sussex does not lie on the downs but is the summit of Black Down (919ft/280m), a greensand ridge that extends southwards like a tendril from Haslemere and the Devil's Punchbowl. The same sandstone underlies Ashdown Forest and the sandy heaths close to Midhurst, giving a type of walking through heather and gorse that is surprising - sometimes in these parts there is the scenic flavour of a grouse moor.

Elsewhere, Wealden landscape predominates: countryside underlain by clay that was originally a vast oak forest. It formed a natural obstacle to progress northwards from the coast until the Romans built roads through it from Chichester and Lewes. Settlement followed, but even in Norman times the forest was still largely intact. In late medieval times, however, the oak trees began to be felled for charcoal that fuelled furnaces and made metal from local ironstone. The industry flourished for nearly four centuries and provided the iron cannons that fired on the Armada. Small streams flowing swiftly through steep-sided valleys provided power for the ironmasters' hammers, and it was only with the discovery of techniques for smelting with coal that the industry ended.

In the 17th and 18th centuries yet more mature trees were cut down for the admiralty when there was urgent need for new battleships to face hostile Dutch and French fleets. Although royal decrees were issued to preserve the best timber for shipbuilding, oak continued to be used as a building material as well. However, many of the timber-framed cottages to be seen in the district also have ancient beams salvaged from medieval dwellings. The oak woodland that survives is surprisingly extensive and provides a welcome contrast to the open countryside of the downs, although the paths are often muddy in winter.

At the time of writing the South Downs has just received its designation as a National Park.

Buildings in the landscape

There are quite a few places in the open countryside of Sussex where you can look around from high ground and see no evidence of human habitation. An expert looking at the scene, however, would probably spot that 3,000 years ago a fortified settlement occupied a ridge on the horizon or that the muddy ponds on the far side of a field in the middle distance are the remains of a moat that surrounded an early medieval manor house. Usually the evidence of human activity is obvious – a compact village lying in the lee of the downs, thatched cottages huddling around an ancient church or an isolated barn built 200 years ago that has recently been expensively converted into a weekend retreat.

The demand for traditional cottages in the depths of the Sussex countryside exploded as more and more people acquired cars. In the 1960s and '70s beautiful black and white or pantiled cottages could be bought for a few hundred pounds. Today, the same properties are worth half a million. The upside of this is that the formerly half-derelict cottages are now in immaculate repair, while the downside is that many are empty for much of the year at a time when there is little affordable accommodation in country towns and villages for local people.

The domestic architecture of the county is probably its most memorable treasure. In towns and villages there is a diversity of style in house and cottage unmatched elsewhere in the kingdom. A medieval timber-framed cottage, with its thatched roof and exposed beams, can be flanked by a weather-boarded house of the 1830s on one side and a slightly later pantiled cottage on the other. Elsewhere in the same street, there may well be handsome Georgian and Regency houses standing close to modern, architect-designed developments

A wealth of beautiful churches provide another valuable legacy. Important for their historical and architectural interest, they also enhance the scenery of the county. However, a church does not have to be of great age to play its part in the landscape. A tower and a red roof in a vista features in many a watercolour on view in the galleries of Rye or Brighton. Visitors will also enjoy seeing grander ecclesiastical buildings like Chichester Cathedral and Battle Abbey, but the village churches seem to epitomise the rare beauty of Sussex, which is essentially intimate.

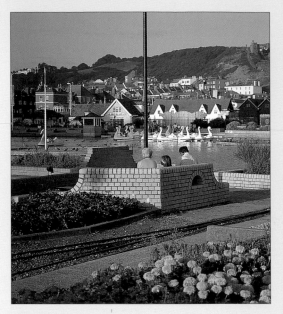

Hastings

At Arundel the county has a fairytale castle, while the castles at Bodiam and Herstmonceux are hardly less romantic. The Normans realised that their successful invasion might be copied by their enemies and took steps to secure the coastline by building castles at strategic positions, both on the coast and in the hinterland. When a Napoleonic invasion was threatened, Martello towers were constructed along the coast and a canal was dug through Romney Marsh so that troops could be speedily moved to vulnerable points. During the Second World War the Sussex coast was recognised as being particularly vulnerable, and some of the pillboxes built then remain as another reminder of a turbulent history.

Practical walking

Experienced walkers know how to adopt routes to suit prevailing conditions. It is not much fun to walk along a cliff edge or along the crest of the downs into a biting east wind or even into the face of a moist westerly. On hot days the cooling breezes on the top of downland are welcome but there is little shade to be found. In winter, tracks through woodland may become waterlogged or even impassable if used by horses. This is fair enough if they are designated as bridleways but annoying if they are footpaths that are theoretically barred to riders.

When you are walking in the countryside there are any number of 'if onlys' that can occur. For example, 'if only I had remembered to bring a knife to scrape mud from my boots' or 'if only I had secateurs in the rucksack to cut those brambles away from the stile'. Brambles, as well as nettles, can also be a problem if you walk barelegged. On most downland routes you are unlikely to encounter much dense vegetation, but once you venture along canal or riverbanks or through woodland you may well be in trouble if you are in shorts or skirt.

It is often amusing to find footprints from trainers deeply etched into puddles of mud. Of course these prints may have been made by cross-country runners but it is more likely that they are those of walkers who have approached the countryside in too casual a manner and been caught out. It is always advisable to wear walking boots if you are embarking on a country walk of reasonable length. They give support if your foot lands badly on a stone or piece of wood. A badly twisted ankle is an emergency in lonely country. For this reason it is probably advisable to carry a mobile phone, but note that there are pubs that will fine you if you receive or make a call on their premises.

Wayfaring should not be a problem on these walks if you follow the mapping correctly. However, there may be occasions where a compass will prove useful, especially walking through woodland on vague paths or if you cross large fields where the far side is below the skyline. It is essential to take a rudimentary first-aid kit and, in summer, sunblock against the surprising strength of the Sussex sun. Some of the walks stay in remote country for all of their length and for these particularly you will need to carry food and drink. Use your camera to record any obstructions or vandalism. Letters to rights of way officers detailing incidents carry weight if pictorial evidence comes with them.

It only remains for the authors and publisher to wish you good walking in Sussex.

With the introduction of 'gps enabled' walks, you will see that this book now includes a list of waypoints alongside the description of the walk. We have included these so that you can enjoy the full benefits of gps should you wish to. Gps is an amazingly useful and entertaining navigational aid, and you do not need to be computer literate to enjoy it.

GPS waypoint co-ordinates add value to your walk. You will now have the extra advantage of introducing 'direction' into your walking which will enhance your leisure walking and make it safer. Use of a gps brings greater confidence and security and you will find you cover ground a lot faster should you need to.

For essential information on map reading and basic navigation, read the *Pathfinder Guide Map Reading Skills* by outdoor writer, Terry Marsh (ISBN 978-0-7117-4978-8). For more information on using your gps, read the *Pathfinder Guide GPS for Walkers*, by gps teacher and navigation trainer, Clive Thomas (ISBN 978-0-7117-4445-5). Both titles are available in bookshops or can be ordered online at www.totalwalking.co.uk

Durford Heath and Rogate Common

Start	National Trust car park, Durford Heath (inconspicuous entrance on the south side of the road to Rogate, close to B2070 at Hill Brow)
Distance	3½ miles (5.6km)
Approximate time	2 hours
Parking	At start
Refreshments	The Jolly Drover at Hill Brow
Ordnance Survey maps	Landranger 197 (Chichester & The South Downs), Explorer 133 (Haslemere & Petersfield)

GPS waypoints

- 🖉 SU 790 259
- Ⓐ SU 787 250
- Ⓑ SU 787 239
- Ⓒ SU 794 240
- Ⓓ SU 799 242
- Ⓔ SU 796 251
- Ⓕ SU 793 255

A short walk mainly through woodland that uses part of the Sussex Border Path on the northern edge of West Sussex. The return leg is mainly uphill, but there are few taxing gradients and the going is mainly over good ground (though note the warning about brambles and nettles after point Ⓑ – it would be unwise to wear shorts). Look out for birds such as green woodpeckers, goldcrests and greenfinches.

Durford's only claim to fame was its abbey, a Premonstratensian house of the 11th century situated near Rogate village. When it was dissolved in 1539, Henry VIII's commissioner found it 'The

Weather-boarded cottage near Durford

poorest abbey I have seen – far in debt and in decay'.

🖉 Go through the pedestrian gate into the wood and walk down with a fence to the right past rhododendrons. Near the National Trust sign at the bottom, fork left to follow the waymarked Sussex Border Path on a sandy path that descends gently through pine trees.

The Sussex Border Path is a challenging long-distance trail that covers 152 miles (245km) between Emsworth and Rye. It more or less follows the boundary of the Saxon kingdom of Sussex, taking in parts of Hampshire, Surrey and Kent as well.

There is another track to the right that runs alongside for some distance. Keep ahead at Long Bottom, where another path crosses your route. Stay

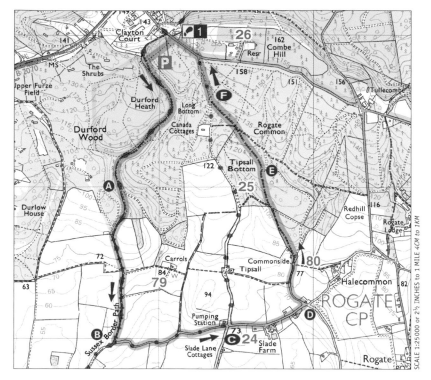

SCALE 1:25 000 or 2½ INCHES to 1 MILE 4CM to 1KM

| 0 | 200 | 400 | 600 | 800 METRES | 1 |
| 0 | 200 | 400 | 600 YARDS | | ½ |

KILOMETRES
MILES

on the Border Path, which continues to descend as the track to the right veers away.

Take the right fork when the track divides **A**. The path climbs out of conifers and there are views over rolling countryside before the path joins with a track from the right. At the bottom of a dip the track, still part of the Sussex Border Path, crosses a footpath. Keep ahead to climb the hill and pass the drive to the left that goes to Carrols.

Where the track swings to the right and begins to descend steeply **B** take the sunken lane on the left. Here brambles snatch at clothing but the romantic character of bygone Sussex survives, when many roads and lanes were like this. The illusion is only slightly marred by the A272 being two fields away to the right. If horses have not used the track recently, nettles may prove to be as troublesome as the brambles. Fork right when a bridleway goes to the left to reach a lane by a pumping-station **C**.

Keep ahead along the lane to pass Slade Farm. Continue for 80 yds (73m) past the picturesque thatched and weatherboarded cottage at Little Slade, then turn left at the junction **D**. Make a short climb up the lane to Commonside. After Commonside House, keep to the bridleway, which bears left into the woods and begins a steady climb. There is a fine view to the south-west just before another bridleway joins from the left. Keep ahead into the pine trees, until the gradient eases at a half-hidden bridleway fingerpost on your left.

E Fork left here, and continue through the thick undergrowth. Cross the track to Canada Cottages at an oblique bridleway crossing, and continue climbing to the five-way junction near Long Bottom.

F Keep ahead onto the major track and turn left at the road. From here it is 300 yds (274m) back to the start. ●

Battle – 1066 Country Walk

		GPS waypoints
Start	Battle Abbey gate	
Distance	3½ miles (5.6km)	TQ 748 158
Approximate time	2 hours	Ⓐ TQ 742 154
		Ⓑ TQ 737 149
Parking	Car park next to abbey	Ⓒ TQ 741 139
Refreshments	Pubs and tearooms at Battle	Ⓓ TQ 744 140
Ordnance Survey maps	Landranger 199 (Eastbourne & Hastings), Explorer 124 (Hastings & Bexhill)	Ⓔ TQ 743 147

This is a delightful short walk given extra interest in that it covers ground where fighting took place on October 14, 1066. The longer trail taking this name extends from Rye to Pevensey, a distance of 31 miles (50km).

After his victory at the Battle of Hastings in 1066 King William gave thanks by founding an abbey at Battle, the high altar being erected at the spot where Harold fell. The site has belonged to English Heritage since 1976 when it was generously given to this country by the citizens of the United States in celebration of the centenary of their nation. Visitors can view the battlefield from the high ground now occupied by the abbey which was the position held by the Saxon army. The stream at the bottom of the little valley takes its

Battle Abbey Gatehouse

reddish colour from iron in the bedrock, though tradition has it that this commemorates the blood shed in the conflict. Once the abbey was established a town grew up around it, steadily increasing in size and prosperity as the monastery itself became increasingly rich and powerful.

📝 Leave the car park by the abbey and turn left down a short lane that ends at a gate. Go through the gate and bear left to continue on the track that follows the fence around the wooded grounds of the abbey. When the path splits **A**, keep right following the 1066 Country Walk. The path drops down towards woods.

After a pleasant stretch through conifers you come to a gate just before a cottage. There is a stile on the left 20 yds (18m) farther on **B**. Go over the stile and cross a meadow to a stile into the wood. The path drops to a lake. You will see from the map that the Powder Mills Hotel is close by. Its name is taken from the gunpowder industry established in Battle in 1676 which lasted for almost 200 years before closing as fear grew for the safety of the town.

Cross the bridge at the outlet and climb ahead following a 'short walk' waymark. A short length of concrete track leads steeply uphill. At the top continue ahead to the road and cross it to the drive to Millers Farm.

Enjoy the views over lovely countryside, walking on the drive past an oast and farmhouse. After Badger's Keep, go through two galvanised

gates **C**, keep left along the front of the house and make for a stile ahead in the far boundary. Turn right and go down the pasture to a bridge and stile. Keep ahead on a bank that takes the path to a bridleway. Turn left, pass Stone Cottage **D** and turn left again at a lane to reach a junction. Cross the road carefully to a path opposite that runs above the road and parallel to it. At the top the path crosses a track going into a yard full of agricultural bits and pieces.

E Follow the track through the yard and continue ahead down a gentle slope. Make for some gates and climb by the side of trees to reach the signpost at **A**. Retrace your steps back to the imposing abbey gateway. ●

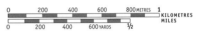

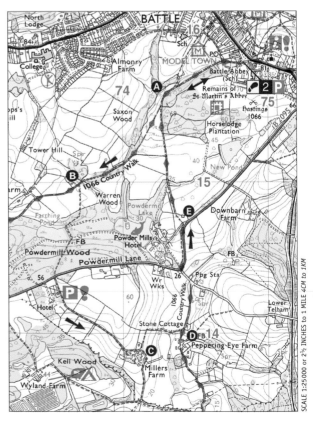

SCALE 1:25000 or 2½ INCHES to 1 MILE 4CM to 1KM

Three Commons Walk

		GPS waypoints
Start	Iping Common car park on west side of Iping to Elsted road, ½ mile (800m) south of A272 at Stedham	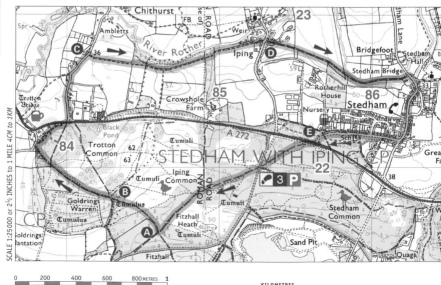 SU 852 219 Ⓐ SU 846 216 Ⓑ SU 842 217 Ⓒ SU 841 227 Ⓓ SU 853 228 Ⓔ SU 856 221
Distance	4 miles (6.4km)	
Approximate time	2 hours	
Parking	At start	
Refreshments	The Keepers Arms at Trotton and the Hamilton Arms at Stedham	
Ordnance Survey maps	Landranger 197 (Chichester & The South Downs), Explorer 133 (Haslemere & Petersfield)	

The sandy commons in the north-west corner of the county provide a habitat for a wide range of birds, plants and insects and are excellent for walking. This route covers three of these commons and, by way of contrast, returns close to the River Rother via the lovely village of Stedham.

Take the bridleway that passes through the car park, leaving it between wooden posts to reach a barrier. Keep ahead, ignoring a Heathland Trail on the left. Heather covers the sandy ground to the left and there is woodland on the right. Nightjars and Dartford warblers are two uncommon species of birds who find this blend of woodland and heath an excellent habitat, which also suits the silver-studded blue butterfly.

Branch right into the wood when the path divides along a banked track. When this emerges from the trees into a grassy area covered with bracken and dotted with silver birch trees, avoid a bridleway on the right and branch half left at the next waymark. The sand underfoot is dazzling, and there are pine trees by the bridleway that give a fragrant scent of resin on a hot day.

Iping Common

The bridleway meets another one in a stand of pines **Ⓐ**. Turn right to walk along a path by rhododendrons (in wet weather you may have to detour slightly to keep dry feet). The bridleway crosses another track before climbing over a stretch of heath to reach a waymark and junction by some trees **Ⓑ**. Keep right here, avoid a turning on the right and descend on a sunken bridleway, following the path alongside Lovehill Cottage. On reaching the road, go forward for a few steps to the Keepers Arms. Both the church at Trotton, which has an outstanding mural of the Judgement, and the bridge over the Rother are medieval.

Return along the road in the direction of the bridleway and take the footpath adjoining it. Climb a slope with a garden to the left and turn left at the top to join a track. Keep ahead on it to reach the A272. Cross the main road to the lane opposite, signposted to Chithurst. This is a village with a monastery, so do not be surprised to see cowled figures in the neighbourhood.

Walk up the lane to reach a row of cottages where the lane bends left. Turn right **Ⓒ** onto a footpath that crosses the ditch by a plank bridge and then follows the edge of a field. Look for a dilapidated stile and walk by woodland where you may see deer. Continue ahead with trees on the left, following the farmland perimeter and farther on enter woodland across a footbridge over a stream. The path swings left to come to a gate on the right. Go through this and along another stretch of field-edge path. Iping village is to the left when you reach a lane, but the walk continues on the bridleway opposite that is cobbled as it climbs from the lane. It joins a drive by Coachman's Cottage.

After 50 yds (46m) leave the drive to the right **Ⓓ**, going through an iron gate (the waymark comes after the gate) and past a luxuriant growth of bamboos. A little farther on and there is a glimpse of the River Rother, flowing 30 or 40ft (9–12m) below. The path descends steadily to Stedham Bridge – pause on the bridge to enjoy the view of the hall and read the notice warning drivers not to leave their locomotives standing on the structure (presumably it would be a convenient place to take on water).

Return from the bridge to walk through Stedham. Turn right at the village sign and pass the school and the Hamilton Arms. Go right **Ⓔ** at the main road and cross it to find a gap in the fence. Descend the bank to the remains of the old main road. A gate takes the bridleway into woodland and then across the heath. Turn left at the road and walk 50 yds (46m) to return to the car park. ●

Cissbury Ring

		GPS waypoints
Start	At the end of the lane that leads from Findon towards Cissbury Ring	✒ TQ 139 085
		Ⓐ TQ 157 081
Distance	4 miles (6.4km)	Ⓑ TQ 159 072
Approximate time	1½ hours	Ⓒ TQ 158 068
		Ⓓ TQ 149 080
Parking	Alternative parking at Storrington Rise off the A24 to the south of Findon village. Follow signed paths to main car park	
Refreshments	None	
Ordnance Survey maps	Landranger 198 (Brighton & Lewes), Explorer 121 (Arundel & Pulborough)	

The walk takes you around the ramparts of Cissbury Ring, one of the most impressive hillforts of southern England. Its defences embrace an area of 65 acres (26 ha), the innermost one being nearly a mile (1.6km) round. The fort dates from about 300BC, though its site was important to neolithic settlers, who mined flint from the hill nearly 3,000 years before.

Most people will approach the start of the walk from Findon, taking the road up the hill through Nepcote Green, the site of the famous sheep fair that has been held since the 13th century. In its heyday 20,000 head of sheep would be driven from all parts of Sussex for the September Fair. It was an immensely colourful event in the first decades of the last century with all sorts of attractions, including a Romany gathering. There was also a Lamb Fair which was held in July, though this seems to have ended in the 1960s.

✒ From the small car park walk towards the gate and National Trust sign for Cissbury Ring. Bear left onto the chalky track that heads eastwards below the defences of the fort. Avoid a bridleway running off half right.

The view towards Worthing from Cissbury Ring

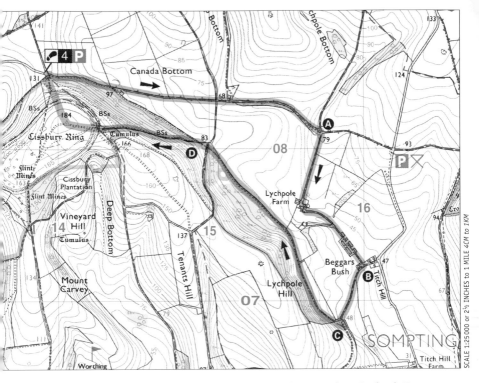

SCALE 1:25000 or 2½ INCHES to 1 MILE 4CM to 1KM

0	200	400	600	800 METRES	1

KILOMETRES
MILES

0	200	400	600 YARDS	½

There are wonderful views of the surrounding downland, but tread carefully as the loose flints underfoot are hazardous to ankles, even if you wear boots.

Keep ahead at Stump Bottom. After this the track divides to make a short, sharp climb. Turn right at the top of this **A**. Lychpole Farm has buildings of finely worked flint, a reminder that flint was mined from Cissbury Hill long before a fort was built on its summit. After the farm, the going is on a concrete track past the modern farm buildings at Beggars Bush. Turn right off the concrete track when it swings sharply left **B** before houses, walking past a tractor shed to an enclosed bridleway. Turn right at a bridleway junction by a gate **C**, go through another gate and turn right to walk through a long meadow. There is a view back to Worthing and the sea.

The path passes above Lychpole Farm and continues with the fence to the right, eventually climbing to a gate at the end of the mile- (1.6km) long meadow. Go through two gates and follow the bridleway ahead. At the National Trust sign **D**, fork left onto the bridleway that begins its steady climb up Cissbury Hill. Cross footpaths that follow the outer defence works to reach the enclosed area at the heart of the fort. There are wonderful views of the coastline and countryside. The chalky soil here supports a host of rare plants, including orchids, which attract 28 species of butterflies. It is hard to imagine an Iron Age township here in 300BC, but it seems likely that the fort was built to defend a permanent settlement.

At the triangulation pillar, turn right and you will see a chalky road that leads away from the car park. Head to the left of this to find steps that take the footpath from the outer ramparts back to the car park. ●

Airman's Grave and Duddleswell

		GPS waypoints
Start	Fairwarp church (on B2026 north of Uckfield)	🖊 TQ 465 267
Distance	3½ miles (5.5km)	Ⓐ TQ 458 274
Approximate time	2 hours	Ⓑ TQ 462 286
Parking	Car park at the church. On Saturdays and Sundays when there are services it may be necessary to start the walk in the village, where there is on-road parking by the green	Ⓒ TQ 469 279 Ⓓ TQ 471 274 Ⓔ TQ 471 269
Refreshments	Duddleswell Tearooms, the Foresters' Arms, Fairwarp	
Ordnance Survey maps	Landranger 198 (Brighton & Lewes), Explorer 135 (Ashdown Forest)	

The first half of this walk in Ashdown Forest is over sandy heath, not at all like a forest. However, the return is through proper woodland, and it is easy to understand why this part of the High Weald is designated an Area of Outstanding Natural Beauty.

Fairwarp is a comparatively new village. When the name was first recorded in 1777 there was just a single farmhouse on the spot, but expansion came in the second half of the 19th century, the church being consecrated in 1881. Although the village remains

The view towards Nutley

active and prosperous, the latter years of the 20th century saw it lose its school and post office. Fortunately, the pub – appropriately the Foresters' Arms – survives.

🖊 The path at the far end of the car park leads to a T-junction. Turn left past the east end of the church and fork right at a grassy area to come to a crossways. Turn left, following the waymark of Maresfield Millennium Footpath. Cross the road to the track going to Spring Garden Farm, bearing to the right through a gate to follow a Millenium Footpath sign. The way across the heath is gloriously colourful at most times of the year with heather, bracken, gorse and birch. Keep ahead at a crossways to leave the Millennium Path and continue ahead at a junction where a farmyard is to the left. The way heads downhill in a north-westerly direction, and Nutley can be seen on the other side of the little valley – there is a Scottish (or at least Peak District) feel to this part of the walk as the path comes to a ford **A**, although the water here is far from that of a pure Highland stream.

Turn right and climb to pass the stone enclosure that protects the grave of the Second Pilot of a Wellington bomber that crashed here on July 31, 1941. The names of the six members of its crew are inscribed on a memorial. From here the path climbs gently to a car park and a road.

B Turn right just before the road, and continue climbing for about 250 yds (229m) past the summit. Fork left along a narrow path through high bracken in season and keep close to the heathland edge, passing stables away to the left. Continue through light woodland to a fork near a metal gate; bear left onto a narrower, more indistinct path, keeping close to the woodland edge on your left until you cross a plank bridge and come to the B2026.

From here the popular Duddleswell Tearooms are just 220 yds (201m) down the road on your right.

Cross this busy main road, and continue down the footpath opposite. Zigzag left and right across the drive to a house, and continue through the woods ahead when the path meets a wider grassy track **C**.

The walking is easy as the track passes a drive on the right, and a 'WW' post on a right-hand bend shows where the Weald Way joins the route **D**.

Pass a white cottage on the left and fork right when the track divides to cross

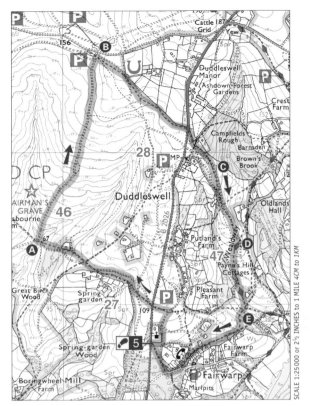

SCALE 1:25000 or 2½ INCHES to 1 MILE 4CM to 1KM

another track after about 100 yds (91m). The track swings right and drops to a shady bridge over a tiny stream. Climb the hill on the other side but, after 50 yds (46m) and just before the brow of the hill, go left **E** on a lesser path, which climbs through bracken and birch. Fork left as the path levels out and comes to a grassy area in front of a white, weatherboarded house. Turn right to walk with the hedge around the next property, close on the left, to reach a path ahead through bracken that soon reaches an unmade road. Join this road, which leads to the village green at Fairwarp.

Turn right and, at the end of the green, go right again on a track past the last houses in the village. After 100 yds (91m) fork left onto a footpath that leads directly to the starting point of the walk at Fairwarp church. ●

Cuckmere Haven from Seaford

		GPS waypoints
Start	Martello Tower Museum, Seaford seafront	
Distance	5 miles (8km)	
Approximate time	2½ hours	
Parking	Near start	
Refreshments	Pubs and cafés in Seaford	
Ordnance Survey maps	Landrangers 198 (Brighton & Lewes) and 199 (Eastbourne & Hastings), Explorer 123 (Eastbourne & Beachy Head)	

GPS waypoints

- ✐ TV 484 984
- Ⓐ TV 487 982
- Ⓑ TV 509 973
- Ⓒ TV 513 976
- Ⓓ TV 504 980
- Ⓔ TV 498 981

There is a climb at the start of this walk but this is steep for only a short way. The summit comes at 226ft (69m) on Seaford Head, where the wonderful coastline of Cuckmere Haven and the Seven Sisters is revealed. The way back is along the northern edge of a nature reserve. Birdwatchers and botanists will appreciate varied habitats that attract many unusual species.

✐ Walk eastwards along the seafront from the Martello Tower, which houses a local history museum with displays illustrating the ways of life of previous generations who lived in Seaford. It also offers the opportunity of seeing the interior of one of the forts built against the threat of Napoleonic invasion. This is Tower No. 74, the westernmost of the 103 that begin at Aldeburgh, in Suffolk, and end here. There is a good view of the chalky ledges of Seaford Head as you approach the beginning of the cliff path Ⓐ.

Look for the sign for the long-distance Vanguard Way and climb the steps to the top of Seaford Head, keeping fencing on the right. The effort is quite strenuous but the views and sense of space improve with every step. Keep in a general easterly direction and look back at the town when you take a breather. It was a thriving port until

1573, when a storm threw up a shingle ridge and diverted the River Ouse northwards. Its fortunes revived in the 19th century when the railway arrived and several large hotels were built. The last of these establishments closed

about 30 years ago.

Seaford Head gives a wonderful view of the Seven Sisters – Haven Brow is the nearest and highest of the cliffs at 253ft (77m). The cliff-face of Beachy Head (534ft/163m high and not one of the Sisters) is hidden from view on the other side of Birling Gap. The profile of the Sisters, with their plunging slopes, illustrates a feature of the geology of chalk country: dry valleys, here seen in section.

The Seaford Head Nature Reserve covers 303 acres (123 ha) of chalk grassland, saltmarsh and shingle. Fulmars can be seen soaring with the help of the updraft from the cliffs, and the gaps at Short Cliff and Cuckmere Haven are busy with migrating birds, like blackcaps and redstarts, in autumn. They chatter loudly as they search the bushes for a last feed before embarking on their long journeys.

The path descends to Hope Gap **B**, where there is access to the shoreline with its rock pools. Climb the other side of Short Cliff. The chimneys of the cottages at Cuckmere Haven – the

Cuckmere Haven

foreground of countless photographs – come into view. The Haven was once a famous venue with smugglers and remains isolated from public roads.

Turn left onto the drive from the cottages **C**. The view inland is outstanding as you climb South Hill. Pass South Hill Barn and bear left **D** to walk with the hedge to the right. There is a concrete drive to the left at first but this diverges. A wooden signpost tells that Seaford is 1½ miles (2.4km) away, even though its outskirts sprawl below.

Follow the waymark right after an enclosed section of path and descend to emerge on downland. Keep ahead when the path divides **E**, following a waymark. The final section is in the same direction (north-west) across the golf course, the path ending at the intersection of Chyngton Road and Southdown Corner. Turn left onto the latter and then right into Corsica Road (perhaps named because the model for Martello towers was the Corsican fort at Mortella). Corsica Road then takes you back to the seafront via Cliff Gardens. ●

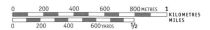

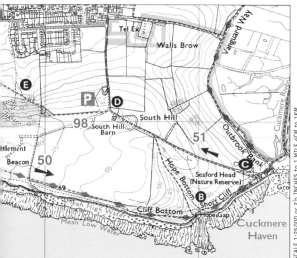

SCALE 1:25000 or 2½ INCHES to 1 MILE 4CM to 1KM

Ardingly Reservoir

		GPS waypoints
Start	Ardingly Reservoir car park (locked at 18.00 in summer, earlier in other months)	🖉 TQ 334 287
		Ⓐ TQ 334 290
Distance	5 miles (8km)	Ⓑ TQ 340 298
Approximate time	2½ hours	Ⓒ TQ 340 304
		Ⓓ TQ 339 308
Parking	At start	Ⓔ TQ 325 303
Refreshments	Pub at Little London, Ardingly, close to Ⓒ	Ⓕ TQ 333 297
Ordnance Survey maps	Landrangers 187 (Dorking & Reigate) and 198 (Brighton & Lewes), Explorer 135 (Ashdown Forest)	

Ardingly (pronounced 'Arding-lye') Reservoir was constructed in 1978 and its 9½ mile (15km) perimeter embraces 198 acres (80 ha). The walk follows the quiet shoreline on the north side of the reservoir and also goes through Tilgate Wood, where a long footbridge spans its major arm. It is a fine place to watch kingfishers, herons and grebe. It is also possible to lengthen the walk with a visit to Loder Valley Nature Reserve (see details below). There may be deep mud towards the end.

🖉 Bear right across the foot of the dam from the information panels, climbing gently to the kissing-gate at the start of the Kingfisher Trail. Continue for 200 yds (183m) to a stile on the right.

Ⓐ Turn right over the stile. The path begins by following the hedge on your right, then climbs across an open field to the signposted crossways at Townhouse Farm; look back here for a fine view of the reservoir and the Ouse Valley railway viaduct. Bear slightly right along a farm track, and keep ahead onto the tarred lane at Hunter's Gate. Pass Ardingly's lovely church with its ancient yew tree, turn right at the junction, and continue for a few paces more.

Ⓑ Turn left onto the short footpath opposite Jordan's Cottage; then, at the wicket gate, turn left onto the drive that skirts the perimeter of the agricultural showground. After about ½ mile

(800m) this swings to the right, and you can follow it in this direction to the pub, appropriately named the Gardeners' Arms as it stands close to the Royal Botanic Gardens at Wakehurst Place. One wing of the house, built by Sir Edward Culpeper in 1590, is incorporated into the existing mansion that was enlarged by the first Lord Wakehurst in 1900. In 1963 it became a National Trust property and was subsequently leased to the Royal Botanic Garden and acquired its nickname 'Kew in the country'.

Ⓒ Otherwise, fork left here through a metal gate into the woodland and follow the path to a T-junction.

Ⓓ Turn left onto a farm drive that descends past a duckpond before the right of way bypasses Tillinghurst farmyard. After a stile by a metal gate, keep the trees to the right and drop down through the meadows. Continue

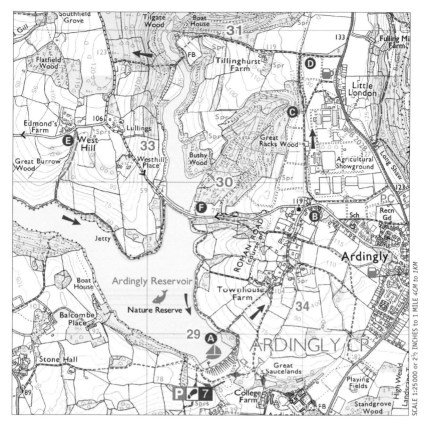

SCALE 1:25 000 or 2½ INCHES to 1 MILE 4CM to 1KM

0	200	400	600	800 METRES	1
					KILOMETRES
					MILES
0	200	400	600 YARDS	½	

past another stile and metal gate to follow a wire deer fence near the bottom. A picnic area beyond the fence heralds a stile. Cross over and turn left, following the woodland track as it bears right past a gate into the Loder Valley Nature Reserve and onto the long wooden footbridge over the northern arm of the reservoir. (Fifty permits each day are available in advance from the office at Wakehurst Place [tel. 01444 894066] for those wishing to explore the secret paths through Bushy Wood, or, on the far side of the bridge, Tilgate Wood. No dogs are allowed.)

Bear right after the bridge to begin climbing the steeply wooded slopes to a lane. Turn left to lose the height that you have just gained (though in compen-sation the lane is hardly less beautiful than the previous path), and turn right at a T-junction towards Balcombe.

E Turn left through the metal gate opposite Edmond's Farm onto a bridleway that follows close to the hedge to the right (do not be tempted by the field track). The bridleway descends a steep coomb into a narrow meadow that has trees on each side and a stream in the middle. The going may get difficult near the bottom where deep mud often surrounds the gap in the hedge. At the foot of the hill turn left through a wicket gate and follow the bridleway along the shoreline as far as the causeway. Now turn right along the roadside path for 220 yds (201m).

F Turn right through the kissing-gate to rejoin the shoreline path, and follow it all the way back to the car park at the foot of the dam. ●

The Chidham Peninsula

		GPS waypoints
Start	Chidham	🖋 SU 793 034
Distance	5 miles (8km)	**Ⓐ** SU 796 034
Approximate time	2½ hours	**Ⓑ** SU 789 020
Parking	Cobnor Farm amenity car park at south end of village	**Ⓒ** SU 780 046
		Ⓓ SU 787 043
Refreshments	The Old House at Home, Chidham	
Ordnance Survey maps	Landranger 197 (Chichester & The South Downs), Explorer 120 (Chichester)	

Chidham faces Bosham across one of the innumerable creeks of Chichester harbour. The footpath that follows the shore of the peninsula takes the walker through a watery landscape whose loneliness is enjoyed by a variety of mud-loving seabirds: curlew, dunlin and redshank in winter and terns, oystercatchers and redshanks in summer. Sections of the walk may be difficult at times of exceptionally high tide.

🖋 Take the path from the car park that heads eastwards towards the shore, following the edge of a field. There's a lovely view of Bosham and its church ahead on the left as you walk towards the flood bank.

Ⓐ Turn right at the fingerpost and walk along the flood bank towards Cobnor Point; herons often fish the

Cobnor Point

lagoons on the landward side of this path. Keep left at the next fingerpost, continuing along the flood bank until you reach the jetty where the path leaves the shore to skirt the Cobnor House Activity Centre. The path is surfaced for wheelchairs when it regains the shore.

There are good views across the channel to West Itchenor as the path turns westwards to round Cobnor Point. It leaves the low cliff for the beach soon afterwards and comes to a mud spit with the remains of old piling **Ⓑ**. The spit is an important nesting-site for seabirds (notably three species of tern), and the piling was put here in the 19th century when an attempt was made to reclaim a wide tract of land from the sea. Before that there was a tidal mill here.

Stunted oak trees stand below a low cliff as the path along the beach swings gradually to the north. It may be tempting to resume walking on the flood wall but *be warned that the long* grass conceals crevices that could easily break an ankle. Thorney Island lies across the water, its ancient church standing among military installations that have become redundant. Similarly, the concrete sea defences along this part of the Chidham Peninsula seem a waste of effort, uprooted and shattered by the power of the sea.

Prinsted church can be seen ahead as the right of way approaches Chidham Point. After passing an area of scrub and a small tidal lagoon, descend the bank by steps **C** and head back below it for 100 yds (91m) before turning left to follow a hedge. Turn right when you reach the lane and walk past the large cream-painted Chedeham House.

D *Keep straight on here to visit*

Chidham's unusually named 17th-century inn, the 'Old House at Home'. Otherwise turn left onto the footpath immediately after the house and, 50 yds (46m) farther on, keep ahead at the three-way junction. Go straight on when you rejoin the lane; then, just after the tiny church with its whitewashed porch, turn left onto a lovely grassy footpath that winds past Chidmere Pond. The pond is mainly screened by trees, but there are a few glimpses across the water to Chidmere Farm just before you reach another lane. Turn right and walk for another 100 yds (91m) back to the car park. ●

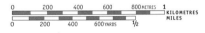

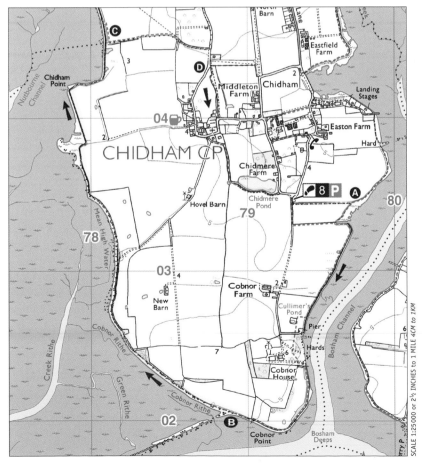

Bewl Water from Wadhurst

		GPS waypoints
Start	Wadhurst	🥾 TQ 641 317
Distance	5½ miles (8.9km)	Ⓐ TQ 644 319
Approximate time	2½ hours	Ⓑ TQ 654 324
Parking	Either of public car parks in the village, one with its entrance by the White Hart, the other next to the Greyhound	Ⓒ TQ 664 325 Ⓓ TQ 666 328 Ⓔ TQ 669 329
Refreshments	Pubs and tearooms in Wadhurst	Ⓕ TQ 663 318 Ⓖ TQ 656 312
Ordnance Survey maps	Landrangers 188 (Maidstone & Royal Tunbridge Wells) and 199 (Eastbourne & Hastings), Explorer 136 (The Weald, Royal Tunbridge Wells)	

Bewl Water is the largest area of open water in the south of England – there is a 13-mile (21km) walk around its perimeter. This walk takes in part of its less-frequented southern shore. Be sure to wear waterproof footwear as the approach path is often wet. It is not advisable to wear shorts on this route.

Wadhurst is one of those places that seems unable to decide whether it is a village or a town (having been granted a charter and a market by Henry III in 1253 it could well claim to be a town). Iron-smelting from local ironstone was probably established when the Romans first came here. In the 17th and 18th centuries Wadhurst prospered from ironfounding – look inside the church to see 31 memorials of cast iron set into the floor. The spire of the church is 128ft (39m) high and, as this walk shows, is a distinctive landmark.

🥾 Walk down Blacksmith's Lane, opposite the Greyhound inn and, when it turns sharply left Ⓐ, keep ahead on the drive to Little Pell Farm. Go through the farmyard and join a track with a hedge to the left that descends to a wood and a muddy pond. Bewl Water can be seen ahead.

The reservoir came into operation in 1975 and holds 31,300 million litres of water. It has become famous for its recreational facilities, catering for fly-fishers, windsurfers, yachtsmen and canoeists as well as walkers and cyclists.

The footpath continues through woodland and between fields, eventually reaching a stile made from an old railway sleeper. Turn right immediately beyond it at a junction with a bridleway Ⓑ. Although this right of way closely follows the shore of the reservoir, there are, as yet, only glimpses of it. Cyclists also use this path and may approach quickly and silently from the rear. After some distance of skirting muddy creeks, the bridleway bursts out into open countryside and a great expanse of Bewl Water is revealed.

Continue along the shore path – if you look back you will see the spire of Wadhurst church rising above the trees. On reaching a small fisherman's hut, turn right onto a bridleway. At the end of the 18th century this isolated district

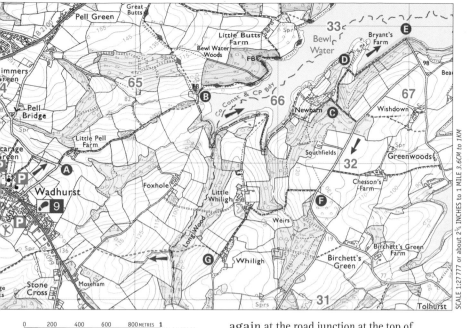

SCALE 1:27 777 or about 2¼ INCHES to 1 MILE 3.6CM to 1KM

0	200	400	600	800 METRES 1
				KILOMETRES
				MILES
0	200	400	600 YARDS	½

was famous for its enormous oak trees, among the last remaining from the forest that once covered the Weald. They provided timber for the fighting-ships that sailed under Nelson's command during the wars against France. The difficulties in removing the trees to the dockyards at Chatham and Portsmouth can only be imagined.

The path leaves the shore to skirt the wood behind the farm and oasthouse at Newbarn. Turn right at a lane and, after 50 yds (46m), take the concrete drive on the left **C** that leads towards Bryant's Farm. At the gateway to the farm, take the footpath to the right **D** down some steps and through woodland. There is a nicely sited seat and another fisherman's hut overlooking Bewl Water and a series of fish tanks used for rearing some of the 50,000 trout that are needed each year to restock the lake.

Turn right **E** onto the lane that (in the other direction) disappears beneath the water of the reservoir. Go right

again at the road junction at the top of the hill and walk along the quiet lane for almost a mile (1.6km), climbing at first. Pass the lane to Chesson's Farm on the left. Less than ¼ mile (400m) farther on where the lane begins to bend left, take the footpath on the right **F** that follows a hedge to the bottom of the field. Turn left after passing two fine oaks to go through a gate and across a bridge. A track takes the route to Little Whiligh. Turn left along the drive to see Wadhurst church on the skyline again.

When a drive rises on the left to Whiligh stableyard, descend the steps on the right **G** and go through a kissing-gate. The path follows the hedge down at first but veers left after a hawthorn tree towards a stile in the fence at the bottom. A grassy path leads to a gate and a bridge over a stream of reddish water. Walk up the edge of a large field with fence, trees and hedge on the left. In the top corner exit to a lane, cross over and go diagonally across this pasture to reach the B2099 at Stone Cross. Turn right here and follow the pavement into Wadhurst. ●

Wolstonbury from Hurstpierpoint

Wolstonbury from Hurstpierpoint

		GPS waypoints	
Start	Hurstpierpoint	✎ TQ 281 165	
Distance	5½ miles (8.9km)	Ⓐ TQ 276 164	
Approximate time	3 hours	Ⓑ TQ 271 156	
Parking	Car park on north side of main street – 4 hour limit	Ⓒ TQ 277 143	
		Ⓓ TQ 284 135	
Refreshments	Pubs, restaurants and tearooms in Hurstpierpoint	Ⓔ TQ 290 139	
		Ⓕ TQ 288 146	
Ordnance Survey maps	Landranger 198 (Brighton & Lewes), Explorer 122 (Brighton & Hove)	Ⓖ TQ 284 150	
		Ⓗ TQ 283 156	

Wolstonbury Hill, capped by an oval-shaped Iron Age Fort, is one of the best viewpoints of the South Downs, so choose a clear day for the walk. The route passes through fields and meadows on the way to Wolstonbury, and there is quite a climb to the 676ft/206m summit. The return goes past Danny, a manor house dating from c. 1580.

Hurstpierpoint is a quiet village just off the London to Brighton road with many attractive Georgian and early-Victorian houses. The church dates from 1843 and was built to plans by Sir Charles Barry, famous for his designs of the Houses of Parliament.

✎ Take the Brighton road (B2117) southwards from the village centre – the church and war memorial are to the right. After 150 yds (137m), by the speed limit sign, take the bridleway to the right. At a crossways, go through the kissing-gate ahead and walk along the field edge to its midway point Ⓐ.

Turn left to cross the field to a solitary oak tree with a squeeze stile close by. Cross the next field diagonally and then turn left by a fringe of trees and reach a footbridge at the top corner of a long meadow. Turn right to join a farm track heading towards Wanbarrow

Farm (and the noise of traffic) and then left onto a concrete drive.

Keep ahead to the footpath junction 200 yds (183m) beyond the farm.

Ⓑ Turn left, then keep ahead when the chalky track turns to the right. Continue across two fields to the B2117, cross the road, and walk up Bedlam Street for 100 yds (91m). Follow the tarmac drive as it turns to the right, and carry on past Randolph's Farm with its high brick chimneys, keeping the outbuildings to the left. Now follow the track through a series of gates and continue into woodland in the shadow of Wolstonbury Hill.

Pass Foxhole Cottages and after 100 yds (91m) leave the drive to the left Ⓒ onto a field-edge bridleway. When this reaches trees the climbing begins. Cross the bridleway at the top of the woodland onto National Trust land.

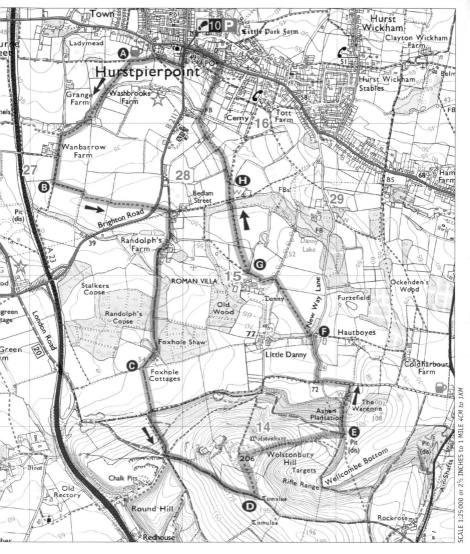

There is a choice of two ascents after about 100 yds (91m). You can either make a direct assault ahead or, slightly less energetically, use a zigzag route. Either way it is a good idea to pause to catch breath occasionally and take in the view to the north to Hurstpierpoint and beyond.

The zigzag route rejoins the bridleway but the gradient is easier around the eastern flank of the hill. As the climbing ends, take the footpath on the left of the track **D** that provides a gentle route to the summit of the hill within the earthen ramparts of the Iron Age fort.

SCALE 1:25000 or 2½ INCHES to 1 MILE 4CM to 1KM

```
0        200      400      600      800 METRES   1
                                               KILOMETRES
                                               MILES
0        200      400      600 YARDS   ½
```

The direct way down to the north (towards Danny mansion) is steep and slippery, and muddy at the bottom. Instead, take the path eastwards so that the ridge of the Downs, and the Jack and Jill windmills, are to the right, and head towards white buildings on the A273 (the nearest one is the pub at Clayton). A stile soon comes into view below. Go over it and keep a dell to the right as you descend to a gate giving onto a bridleway **E** at the bottom of the field. Bear left onto this and then fork right on a footpath past a cottage, called The Warenne, and follow its drive to a lane.

Turn left along the lane and follow it around the right-hand bend as far as the Victorian letterbox beside the drive to Little Danny stables. (The name derives from the Saxon *danegithe*, meaning 'a haven in a valley.')

F Turn left here onto the signposted footpath, crossing a plank bridge and stile into a meadow. The footpath across the meadow gives a good view of the south and east fronts of Danny, an Elizabethan mansion that was remodelled in the time of Queen Anne. During the First World War the house was leased by Prime Minister Lloyd-George and in 1918 the terms of the Armistice were drawn up here by the War Cabinet.

On the far side of the meadow a stile brings you to Danny's drive and entrance gate. Keep ahead here for 100 yds (91m) along the tarmac drive that approaches the north side of the house. Now turn right over a stile, to join the foopath that goes along the edge of the fields and across a plank bridge before dividing at a squeeze stile **G**. Bear right across a meadow and then a field. After a belt of trees there is another plank bridge and then a crossways. Keep ahead across the field and then fork left **H** over a stile, to take an enclosed path that reaches a lane at Little Washbrook Farm. Continue for 150 yds (137m) then turn right onto a waymarked footpath that crosses a footbridge and driveway before climbing to the village green. Turn left at the main street to return to the car park and village centre. ●

Wolstonbury

Herstmonceux

Start	Herstmonceux		GPS waypoints
Distance	5½ miles (8.9km)		✐ TQ 634 125
Approximate time	3 hours		Ⓐ TQ 636 124
Parking	Car park at village centre		Ⓑ TQ 632 117
			Ⓒ TQ 634 113
Refreshments	The Brewers' Arms and The		Ⓓ TQ 639 114
	Woolpack Inn, Herstmonceux		Ⓔ TQ 643 111
Ordnance Survey maps	Landranger 199 (Eastbourne &		Ⓕ TQ 643 102
	Hastings), Explorer 124 (Hastings		Ⓖ TQ 653 103
	& Bexhill)		Ⓗ TQ 647 110

This country walk gives a good view of Herstmonceux Castle, a romantic building dating from 1441 with its towers and turrets reflected in the waters of its moat. The walk covers farmland and woodland in a beautiful part of East Sussex but some of the paths have been neglected and are unmarked, so careful map reading is important.

The parish church and the famous castle are two miles (3.2km) distant from the centre of Herstmonceux both by road and by footpath. The village is famous for its trugs, garden baskets skilfully made of wood, invented here by Thomas Smith, who took samples to London in 1851 and showed them to Queen Victoria at Buckingham Palace. The Trug Shop bearing his name is to be found in Hailsham Road.

✐ From the car park by the Health Centre in the middle of the village, walk to the main road and cross from the Woolpack Inn to take the footpath by the Gardener Street nameboard. The asphalted path climbs on the edge of the playing field. Go through the kissing-gate at the top Ⓐ and bear right towards a lone oak tree. Pass this to reach a kissing-gate in the corner of the field.

Walk with the fence to the left, facing a wonderful view across the Pevensey Levels to the sea and downs. Bear slightly right at the end of the fence to a

metal gate on the far side of the field. Go through here – and the second gate a few paces farther on – and continue across the next field to a kissing-gate. Bear gently left to cross another field to a second kissing-gate. Turn left and then immediately right to pass a tiny overgrown pond Ⓑ and turn left before a metal gate to cross a meadow with another overgrown pond to the left. The discernible path across the meadow takes you to a gap in the hedge. Bear left across the next meadow, heading to the right of a house and drop down to cross a footbridge and stile. Now make for the left side of the garden ahead and cross two stiles before reaching a lane at Butler's Farmhouse.

Cross to the footpath opposite and follow the left-hand edge of a field to a gateway Ⓒ. The right of way crosses the next field diagonally, heading to the left of the house on the far side, though this may be difficult if the path is not cleared. Turn right after a stile to reach the road past a barn and cottage (Little Butlers). Turn left and, after 50 yds (46m), take the field-edge path on the right, descending to a footbridge **D**. However, do not cross this but, 10 yds (9m) before it, go through the small metal gate to the right and cross the plank bridge to follow the field edge down to a small metal gate on the left of a drainage ditch. Continue through the gate and, 20 yds (18m) farther on, go through a metal field gate, then follow the track uphill to a stile and gateway visible on the skyline. Look to the right for a fine view of Herstmonceux Place with its classical

façade. After the stile **E** turn right onto a bridleway and walk down by the hedge to the bottom of the dip. Do not follow the track to the right but keep ahead and climb the steep slope to a metal gate by a birch tree. A pleasant stretch of level woodland walking follows. Keep ahead when a footpath crosses and bear left when you reach Church Road.

Pass the church and turn left onto a bridleway **F** that is part of the 1066 Country Walk. This crosses the driveway to the Observatory (Herstmonceux Castle was the headquarters of the Royal Greenwich Observatory for 40 years until it was acquired by Queen's University, Canada, in 1993, which established the International Study

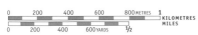

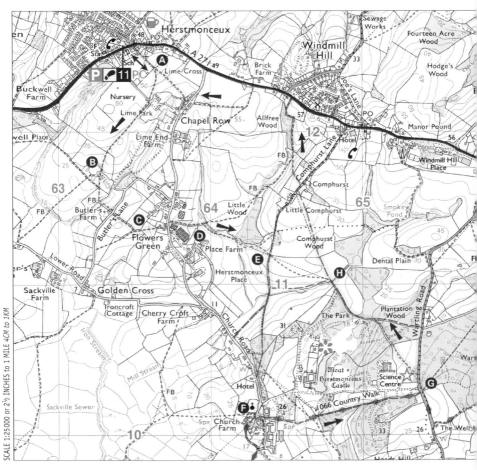

Herstmonceux Castle

Centre). On the other side of the drive the path soon emerges from woodland to give an excellent view of the south side of the moated castle. Remarkably, much of this is fairly modern – rebuilding took place in 1912. The original interior had been stripped at the end of the 18th century to provide building material for Herstmonceux Place. However, the exterior survives and is notable for being one of the largest castles of its date in the country, and the first to be built of brick.

The pleasant walking continues along the bridleway to reach a road near the drive to the Science Centre. Turn left and, after 100 yds (91m), go left over a stile **G** and walk diagonally across the field. After a stile in the far corner, the path descends through Plantation Wood and bears left onto a track that passes between the park's two lakes. There is a good view of Herstmonceux Place to the left when this bridleway emerges into open country.

H Keep straight on, making for a point roughly between the two houses in the trees on the skyline. Go through a metal gate, and keep ahead until you

reach Comphurst Lane. Turn right, and follow the lane for 100 yds (91m). Cross the stile on the left opposite the entrance to Comphurst itself and follow the footpath across two meadows to reach a stile by Allfree Wood. The windmill on top of Windmill Hill overlooks this pretty valley. Walk up the east side of the wood to the main road and turn left.

After about 300 yds (274m) on the footway, take the footpath on the left and climb for about 160 yds (146m). Now turn right through a small metal gate and make for a point about 50 yds (46m) to the right of the chapel, where another small gate brings you to the former Welcome Stranger at Chapel Row. Despite the encouraging notices on the wall, the old pub is no longer open for business.

Turn left; then, opposite the chapel, take the footpath on the right that initially seems to run in the wrong direction. However, it soon swings left to a kissing-gate. The roof of the sports pavilion passed early in the walk can be seen on the skyline beyond a long meadow. Go through a kissing-gate close to the pavilion to rejoin the path by the side of the recreation ground near the start. ●

Belloc's Mill

		GPS waypoints	
Start	School Lane, Shipley	✏	TQ 143 219
Distance	6 miles (9.7km). Shorter version 5½ miles (8.9km)	Ⓐ	TQ 144 219
Approximate time	3 hours. (2½ hours for shorter version)	Ⓑ	TQ 153 218
		Ⓒ	TQ 155 212
		Ⓓ	TQ 147 213
Parking	Roadside village car park at start, 100 yds (91m) east of mill entrance	Ⓔ	TQ 149 204
		Ⓕ	TQ 151 196
		Ⓖ	TQ 139 196
Refreshments	The Crown Inn, Dial Post; diversion to the Countryman Inn, Whitehall	Ⓗ	TQ 137 207
Ordnance Survey maps	Landranger 198 (Brighton & Lewes), Explorers 134 (Crawley & Horsham) and 121 (Arundel & Pulborough)		

Combine a visit to the King's Mill (bought by the writer Hilaire Belloc in 1906 and the largest working smock mill in Sussex) with an exploration of the surrounding countryside. Some of the bridleways are muddy most of the year so this is not a walk for those wearing trainers. The mill is open and working on the first and third Sundays of the month.

Built in 1879, the King's Mill at Shipley is one of the finest working smock mills in the country. The term comes from the shape of the tower, supposed to resemble the garment traditionally worn by country workers of the time. The fantail, set at right angles to the main sails, moves the cap to keep the sails facing the wind. Belloc lived in Shipley and bought the mill, which continued to work until 1926 – the beginning of the agricultural depression. The author still owned it when he died in 1953, by which time it was in disrepair. The windmill was restored as a memorial to Belloc, and its sails began turning again in 1958.

✏ Turn east along School Lane, then left at the junction into Red Lane. Just beyond King's Platt, the group of modern houses to the right, turn off the

road to the right Ⓐ onto a footpath running down the side of a meadow by the gardens of houses. After 100 yds (91m) go right again through a kissing-gate into a wood. A stile takes the path on into another meadow. Go along the left-hand side to an iron gate giving onto a lane. Cross to a footpath that goes through a belt of trees into a meadow and follow a line of old oak trees in the direction shown by a fingerpost to reach a second fingerpost on the far side. Turn right onto a drive and after 200 yds (183m), by a corner of a wood Ⓑ, leave the drive to the right to cross a large field to reach the main drive coming from Knepp Castle, a gothic fantasy complete with turrets and battlements. The scant remains of its Norman predecessor can be seen by the A24. King John later enjoyed

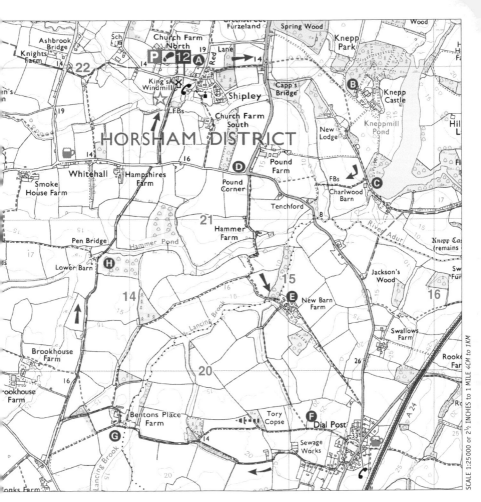

staying at the castle, using it as a
hunting lodge and keeping 200
greyhounds there for pursuing deer.

Turn right onto the drive by an
enormous oak tree and leave the park
by New Lodge. Continue along the drive
for ¼ mile (400m) to take the footpath
to the right **C**, immediately before the
converted Charlwood Barn. However, you
may like to keep on the drive for a few
more yards to see beautiful Kneppmill
Pond to the left before returning to take
the footpath. The pond is one of the
largest hammer ponds in the county
and served Knepp Furnace from 1568
until iron-making ended there in 1604.

The footpath follows the left-hand
side of the field. There are more
magnificent oak trees to the left (a

memorable feature of this walk and
descendants of those that fed the furnace)
and extensive views to the left. Go over
a plank bridge at the corner of the field
and cross a narrow meadow to a more
substantial bridge spanning the River
Adur. Once there was a causeway across
the water meadow here, but only
fragments of timber and brickwork
remain. The clear path continues ahead
across the field – ignore the alternative
to the left – and turn right through the
gate onto Swallows Lane.

Turn left at Pound Corner **D** onto the
footpath that follows a concrete track
towards Hammer Barn. The concrete

King's Mill at Shipley

surface ends at Hammer Farm; follow the gravel lane as it winds on through the farm, then bear left at the next footpath junction and continue to New Barn Farm.

E Turn right opposite an asbestos shed, to pass a pond. Bear left after an iron gate to follow a fingerpost and walk along the edge of a field with a hedge to the left. Continue through a gate along the edge of a much larger field, still following the hedge on your left. Cross the next one to a plank bridge **F** and turn left to Dial Post *(or turn right if you do not wish to visit the village).*

Cross the village green to the main street, turning right to pass the Crown inn. After 150 yds (137m), turn right into Benton's Lane and fork left at Half Acre. Soon habitation is left behind, and the lane becomes a quiet byway.

The short-cut avoiding Dial Post rejoins just before a half-hidden house at the corner of a wood.

The bridleway has now become a lovely green way. At Bentons Place Farm **G** bear right with the fingerpost and pass between the farm and the pond. Follow the track between outbuildings and keep to the bridleway as it bears left, ignoring the footpath right. Pass through the edge of a copse and turn right on reaching a wide bridleway heading north east.

In summer this is the most delightful part of the route with a breathtaking display of wild flowers and butterflies and delicious blackberries. Keep ahead along the broad bridleway (which gradually becomes narrower) until a metal gate across the track heralds the cattle shelter at Lower Barn. Walk past the shelter and turn right into a narrower track **H**. Even in summer the going may be muddy here at times, and in dry conditions the mud becomes well rutted. On reaching the lane, you may like to turn left for a 750-yd (686m) diversion to the Countryman Inn. Otherwise turn right for 50 yds (46m), then left to rejoin the bridleway. Continue across a footbridge to reach Shipley Mill, where you bear left onto the tarmac drive for the return to School Lane. Turn right for the final 100 yds (91m) back to the car park. ●

The Wey and Arun Canal from Billingshurst

The Wey and Arun Canal from Billingshurst

		GPS waypoints	
Start	Billingshurst library		
Distance	6 miles (9.7km)	🖍	TQ 086 260
Approximate time	3 hours	Ⓐ	TQ 072 254
Parking	At start	Ⓑ	TQ 062 244
Refreshments	Pub at Ⓐ; pubs, bistro and	Ⓒ	TQ 058 244
	tearoom in Billingshurst	Ⓓ	TQ 058 245
Ordnance Survey maps	Landranger 197 (Chichester &	Ⓔ	TQ 066 255
	The South Downs), Explorer 134	Ⓕ	TQ 069 271
	(Crawley & Horsham)	Ⓖ	TQ 076 268
		Ⓗ	TQ 080 262

There is hardly anything in the way of a gradient in this interesting walk by the upper reaches of the River Arun. The path runs between the river and an old canal for some of the way, part of the walk aptly named the Kingfisher Trail.

Before the coming of the railway, Billingshurst was a busy staging-post on the road between Bognor and London, and several large inns lined the main street. While the railway dealt an initial blow to the fortune of Billingshurst, it later restored its prosperity when commuters began to settle in and around the village. This development has accelerated in recent years, and the walk sets off through the pleasant modern housing that now reaches out to the A29 bypass.

🖍 Start the walk from the library at Billingshurst, on the west side of the large village that is bisected by the Roman Stane Street. Walk away from the main street and pass to the left of the library. Go left at the crossroads and walk down Frenches Mead to the T-junction. Turn right into West Street, then left at the roundabout into Newbridge Road, and continue across the footbridge over the bypass. Continue along the redundant highway

past Bridgewaters Farm and bear left to join the footpath by the side of the A272. At Lordings Road (B2133) turn left to pass the pantiled Limeburners Inn. About 50 yds (46m) after the pub, turn right Ⓐ on to the drive to Guildenhurst Manor.

After 100 yds (91m) leave the drive to the left through a kissing-gate. A wooden wicket gate now leads you diagonally across a paddock to a gate at its right-hand corner. The enclosed footpath now bears right through a second gate to skirt the next paddock and crosses a footbridge at the corner. From here, follow the signposted zigzag left, then right, and continue down the right-hand edge of the next field to reach a large pond. Turn right, and follow the water's edge around to the left until you cross the concrete bridge over the outlet stream. Bear right after this to follow the new-born River Arun on a delightful path that gives a distant view of the church at Wisborough

Green. Go through a damp meadow full of buttercups to come to a stile beneath electricity lines. Keep ahead for 50 yds (46m) after this, before bearing left **B** to climb with the cables overhead to the top of the wood.

Turn right on to a grassy path that follows the edge of the wood westwards, enjoying the wide view of richly wooded hills with no habitation in sight until Frithwood Farm appears on the left. Continue to skirt the wood as the path drops to a gateway, where the footpath divides **C**. Bear right to follow the path that curves right to reach the footbridge and kissing-gate at Lording's Lock. The Wey and Arun Canal had a life of 101 years, having been opened in 1787. This lock (also known as Orfold Lock) is the top lock of six and from here the barges had to travel another 67 miles (108km) to reach London Bridge. The canal crosses the river on an aqueduct just north of the lock, where an information board explains the details and continuing restoration.

Go over the stile after the lock **D** and turn left to follow the course of the old canal (if you prefer you can follow a meandering riverside path). Parts of the canal are infilled as the right of way cuts across a wide loop of the river. The path continues over a stile and turns left into a muddy, narrow meadow where the path runs between canal and river. After a wooden footbridge, keep ahead **E** – do not cross Guildenhurst Bridge to the right over the Arun – and follow the canal to Newbridge. Note the old crane on the wall of the house by the canal just before the road. Even in its heyday in the 1830s the canal came nowhere near to meeting expectations. Its builders grandly claimed that 130,000 tons of goods would be carried between London and Portsmouth each year but even at the height of its fortunes it only managed some 2,000 tons.

Cross the road and continue by the canal – even if you fail to spot a kingfisher, dragonflies and herons should be seen somewhere along this section. The lift bridge at Northlands Farm does not look as though it is operated often, but the memorial stone close by is poignant – 'a place for kingfishers to rest'.

Turn right **F** at a canal bridge, just before the electricity pylon spanning the canal. Here lock gates have been restored. Cross the River Arun at a sluice and climb

Wey and Arun Canal

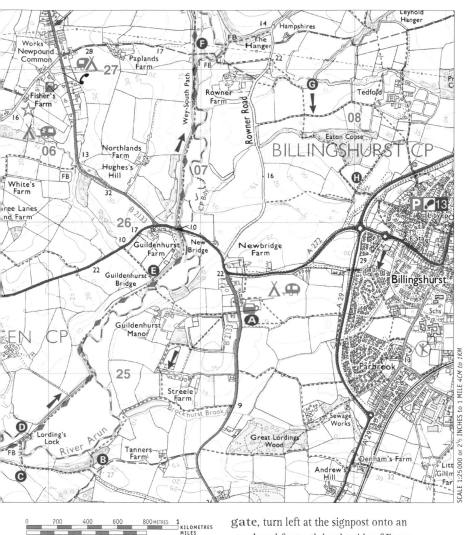

SCALE 1:25000 or 2½ INCHES to 1 MILE 4CM to 1KM

0	200	400	600	800 METRES	1

KILOMETRES
MILES

0	200	400	600 YARDS	½

the track to the top, bearing left through a farmyard to reach Rowner Road. Turn right but, after 30 yds (27m), go left up steps to a stile. Cross a field to stiles and a bridge in the left-hand corner. Turn left and walk along the edge of a field to reach a signpost at a junction by two metal gates. Do not go through the gates but keep the wire fence to the left for 100 yds (91m) to a signpost.

G Turn right across the field to the signpost and stile opposite. Cross a lane and then a meadow; go through a belt of trees and then, before the second gate, turn left at the signpost onto an enclosed footpath by the side of Eaton Copse. Turn right at the footpath sign by the end of the copse and continue through a wooded tunnel for 100 yds (91m). Now turn left over a stile and follow the left-hand hedge down the side of an open field towards new housing.

H At a crossways by trees, where there is a signpost and a stile, keep ahead through woodland to reach the bypass.

Cross the road to the footpath opposite, which passes garages and reaches a road. Turn left towards the church and cross Coombe Hill to return to Billingshurst Library. ●

Rye from Iden

		GPS waypoints
Start	Iden church	☑ TQ 914 237
Distance	6 miles (9.7km)	Ⓐ TQ 914 232
Approximate time	3 hours	Ⓑ TQ 911 219
Parking	Recreation ground car park at start	Ⓒ TQ 912 215
		Ⓓ TQ 916 208
Refreshments	The Bell at Iden, pubs and tearooms in Rye	Ⓔ TQ 925 206
		Ⓕ TQ 932 225
Ordnance Survey maps	Landranger 189 (Ashford & Romney Marsh), Explorer 125 (Romney Marsh, Rye & Winchelsea)	Ⓖ TQ 925 235

Parking is at a premium at Rye in the summer but this walk presents a way of overcoming the problem. Although some of the paths on the route seem to be underused, it gives unusual views of the town and the freedom to take time to explore it fully. At times careful map-reading is needed.

There is a small car park at the recreation ground by All Saints' Church at Iden or, if this is full, there is always adequate on-street parking in the village. Iden wins a mention in *The Guinness Book of Records* as the two rectors who held office from 1807 served 117 years between them, the second one dying in 1924. The sturdy, battlemented tower is the main feature of the church, dating from the 11th century.

☑ Walk past the west end of the church to a group of small oak trees in the corner of the playing field. Here a well-concealed and unwaymarked footpath starts on the left, swinging right to reach a stile. After this it follows the edge of a field with a fence to the left, descending to a plank bridge and stile at the bottom. Follow the waymark to the right and make your way through a 'conservation meadow', planted with uniform lines of fruit trees. Beyond them cross a field, go through a gate and keep left along the field edge

to a stile by an asbestos hut.

Cross a bridleway and the stile on the other side Ⓐ and keep ahead to find a metal stile by a beech tree. Turn right to follow a hedge down to the corner of Tighe's Wood. The path is faint as it leads along the edge of the wood and descends to another metal stile at the end of a row of sweet chestnut trees. The path is more obvious as it climbs with a fence to the left to the A268, meeting the road at a weatherboarded cottage.

Turn left for 20 yds (18m) and then go right on a grassy bridleway, dropping down into a little valley. Make for the field corner and continue on the path when it becomes enclosed by trees and bushes. Pass a path on the left and soon follow the path right into an adjacent field corner Ⓑ. Turn left along the field edge until you see a waymark and swing right across the field, heading uphill towards the boundary.

The steady climb leads you to a gap in the hedge close to the field corner

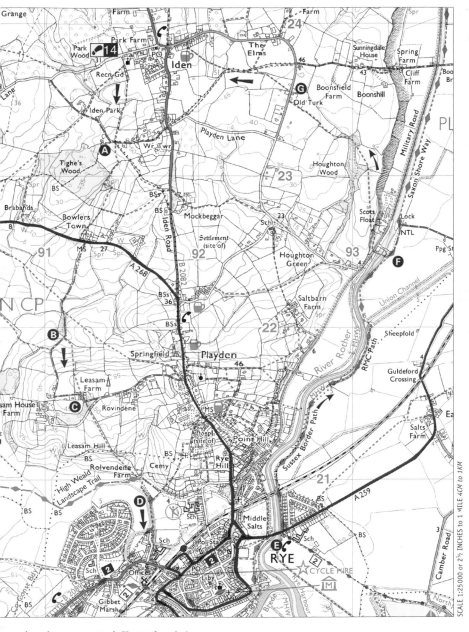

SCALE 1:25000 or 2½ INCHES to 1 MILE 4CM to 1KM

(can be overgrown). Keep ahead along a field edge path to a stile and enter the yard of Leasam Farm. Keep ahead past Leasam Byre and, where the drive swings left, leave it to the right **C** to climb a stile into woodland. Cross an asphalted driveway to a kissing-gate that gives the first view of Rye with its windmill well seen ahead. There is an

even better view from the stile a little way farther down Leasam Hill, at the top of a belt of trees.

Descend to Rolvendene Farm, go through a gate and bear left in front of the farm, then keep right to follow the path along the grassy embankment between the river and the drive. Go right when you reach a surfaced footpath **D** and pass a row of terrace houses before coming to the main road. Turn left to the level crossing and so come to the town centre.

Most people will like to make their own way through Rye with its fascinating old streets and alleys, and equally intriguing and diverse shops and eating places. The route passes through the town from west to east and leaves it by the London road (A259) that crosses the River Rother after a roundabout. Walk along to the road bridge, cross it and then turn left to join the Saxon Shore Way **E**.

The path forms part of the Saxon Shore Way, the Sussex Border Path and the Royal Military Canal footpath. There is little headroom as it goes beneath the railway bridge but after this the walking is enjoyable, with the river and gentle hills to the left and Romney Marsh to the right. Cross the Union Canal and, ½ mile (800m) farther on, turn left to cross the river at Scots Float Sluice **F**.

The approach to Rye

Cross the road to a footbridge on the other side, which forms the start of a path that climbs into a wood, with steps helping the ascent up steep slopes. The stile at the top gives on to a clearly defined path across a large field. Cross the next field diagonally to Houghton Wood. The path goes through the wood, a stream using it in wet weather. After the second of two plank bridges the right of way leaves the trees, crosses the neck of a field and then follows the field edge towards a farmhouse (curiously known as Old Turks).

Go right at the road, then left onto a waymarked footpath opposite Old Turks **G**. Cross the field diagonally to a stile on the left of a metal gate. Keep ahead with a pond to the right, and then follow the boundary hedge, avoiding a waymarked path on the right. Keep to the field edge, then just before reaching a gateway, bear right through a gap in the hedge to follow a path (not waymarked) across the centre of a field to a stile. Continue across the next field to a stile and a narrow path leading to a road. Turn left to a crossroads by the Bell and cross over into Church Lane, following it back to the car park. ●

Icklesham from Winchelsea

Icklesham from Winchelsea

		GPS waypoints	
Start	Winchelsea	🖉	TQ 905 173
Distance	6½ miles (10.5km)	🅐	TQ 908 175
Approximate time	3 hours	🅑	TQ 895 156
Parking	On-street parking in Winchelsea	🅒	TQ 891 156
Refreshments	Pubs and tearoom in Winchelsea,	🅓	TQ 886 159
	pub in Icklesham	🅔	TQ 876 155
Ordnance Survey maps	Landranger 189 (Ashford &	🅕	TQ 879 164
	Romney Marsh),	🅖	TQ 885 162
	Explorer 124 (Hastings & Bexhill)	🅗	TQ 894 162

Winchelsea, like its neighbour Rye, is a town crammed full of history, much of it violent. Its streets follow the grid pattern established by Edward I after the destruction of the old town by a storm in 1287. At the start the walk follows the Royal Military Canal, constructed against the threat of Napoleonic invasion, and after this the going is on field paths and a quiet country lane.

Visitors to Winchelsea come to admire its gracious 18th- and 19th-century houses, tidily arranged around the grid of streets laid out by Edward I after a storm had swept away the old town situated on the shoreline. Quays were built on the River Brede, and Winchelsea grew on its hilltop to become a prosperous walled town with 6,000 inhabitants. It was affiliated to the Cinque Ports but its prosperity eventually proved its downfall, attracting French privateers who raided the town repeatedly and massacred the population. In addition, the river began to silt up so that by the 16th-century Winchelsea had lost its access to the sea, leaving the town stranded on its remote hill.

🖉 The walk starts from the church at the centre of the little town, which was designed as the hub of the 13th-century reconstruction. As can be seen, it was originally a much larger building, only the chancel surviving the

destruction caused by the French pirates. From the church walk eastwards down the high street to pass the tearoom and former post office and continue to come to Strand Gate, one of the three surviving gates into the town (the medieval walls have disappeared). From the gate descend Strand Hill and carefully cross the main road at the bottom. Turn right, pass the Bridge Inn and recross the A259 to the road to Winchelsea Beach.

Cross the Royal Military Canal and take the path on the right 🅐, signposted Cliff End, following the canal's east bank. The canal was excavated in 1804 when the threat of Napoleonic invasion was at its height. It sweeps eastwards in a great arc to Hythe, separating Romney Marsh from inland Kent. It served as a defensive moat and could be used to ferry troops quickly to vulnerable points. There are good views of the town from the banks of the canal and glimpses of the ruins of Greyfriars monastery through the trees.

The going becomes easier after a stile leads to grazing land. Pass a bridge that takes a footpath over the canal and keep to the bank as it begins to swing left. Cross the wooden footbridge at the end of the bend **B**, avoid the concrete bridge on the right and continue alongside the dyke. Go through a gate into the Pannel Valley Nature Reserve and pass a bird hide on the left. Take the next bridge on the right, swing immediately right and then follow the track as it curves to the left between reedbeds to reach an old concrete outbuilding **C**.

Keep ahead uphill towards a house and swing left at the top towards

outbuildings. Turn right on reaching a gate, follow the path over two stiles and cross a drive by a kissing-gate. Go ahead across the field, making for a stile in the right-hand corner, followed by two more stiles. Keep right in the next field and follow the path to a stile leading out to the lane **D**.

Turn left, following the sign to Pett. There is a view to the left over marshes to Dungeness. There are more lovely views as the quiet lane drops down towards Pannel Bridge. Where the lane levels and turns left, take the track on the right to Little Pannel Farm. The right of way passes the front of the garden and then crosses the field to a metal gate at the top corner **E**. Go through it and over the stile and plank bridge on the left. Bear right up the field, heading to the left of a large cattle shed and pass through the farmyard to

0	200	400	600	800 METRES	1
					KILOMETRES
					MILES
0	200	400	600 YARDS	½	

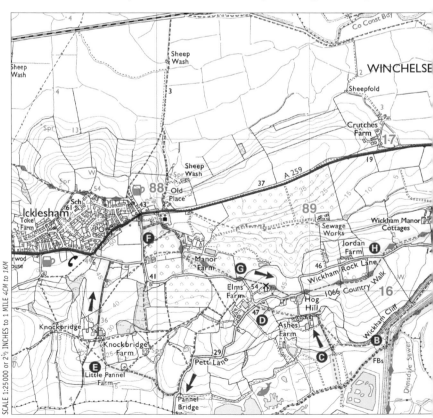

SCALE 1:25 000 or 2½ INCHES to 1 MILE 4CM to 1KM

a farm drive. Turn left at the end on to a lane that soon reaches the A259 at Icklesham.

Turn right and walk through the village. The Queen's Head lies a short distance along Parsonage Lane, a left turning. Opposite the junction is Workhouse Lane. Take this turning and just past the village hall, turn left **F** to follow the 1066 Country waymark. The path passes behind Icklesham church and skirts an orchard before passing to the right of an oast house. Turn left off the asphalted drive to go through the orchard towards the postmill. Note the badger gates through the rabbit fence.

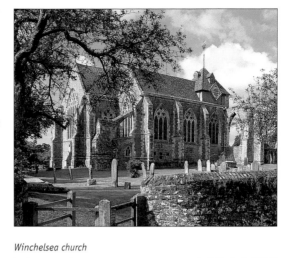

Winchelsea church

Turn left at a lane after leaving the orchard. After 50 yds (46m) go left **G** to cross the meadow behind Icklesham windmill. There is a wonderful view from here. Turn left at a lane, but after 150 yds (137m) keep ahead to climb a stile and cross a field to the edge of trees. The 1066 Country Walk directs you straight across the field. Cross several stiles and cut off the field corner before reaching a lane **H**. Cross it and the stile on the other side. The path runs parallel to the lane to another stile and then crosses the field towards Wickham Manor, a lovely 16th-century house owned by the National Trust. Make for an electricity post to the right of outbuildings and cross stiles and the drive. Now head to the left of New Gate, the southern entry into medieval Winchelsea, to reach the corner of the field, where a stile takes the path over the Town Ditch. Follow the path as it drifts over to the right-hand side of the pasture and begin to approach the field slope. Cross two stiles with a bridleway in between and go uphill towards a ruined building, probably a barn that once belonged to the Friary. Turn right to follow the road to the south side of the churchyard. ●

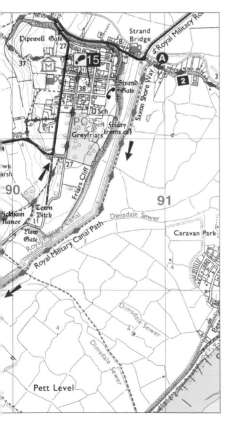

Hastings Country Park

		GPS waypoints	
Start	Visitor Centre, Hastings Country Park, Fairlight		TQ 860 116
Distance	6 miles (9.7km)	**A**	TQ 861 113
Approximate time	3 hours	**B**	TQ 855 115
Parking	At start	**C**	TQ 842 109
Refreshments	None en route but tearoom 200 yds (183m) from start	**D**	TQ 827 096
Ordnance Survey maps	Landranger 199 (Eastbourne & Hastings), Explorer 124 (Hastings & Bexhill)		

It would be a mistake to think that this is a simple stroll through a manicured landscape. In fact the route covers field and woodland as well as downland and cliffs, and the switchback clifftop path on the return is steep in places.

Walk towards the sea from the car park (the upper car park by the toilets serves as a relief one at busy times when the one by the visitor centre is full). There is a fine view eastwards along the coastline to Dungeness. Take the footpath to the right **A** immediately before the former coastguard cottages, waymarked to Fairlight and Warren glens. The clear, well-used path crosses fields and heathland with fine views over towards the coastline. Keep ahead to reach Warren Cottage **B** and beyond it across a meadow. If you have been in touch with the warden, he will no doubt have told you about the amazing variety of wildlife to be seen in the 640-acre (260-ha) park. There are dormice, adders and glow worms here. Dartford warblers are often seen in the gorse bushes, and from the clifftop path dolphins can sometimes be seen leaping from the waves.

A long section of enclosed path ends at a road on a bend. Keep ahead along Barley Lane, follow the 1066 Hastings Walk. Ignore paths on the left and right,

pass a row of cottages and reach a galvanised gate with a path on the right

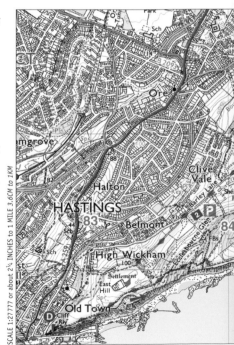

SCALE 1:27777 or about 2¼ INCHES to 1 MILE 3.6CM to 1KM

for Fairlight Road. Avoid it but turn left here ⓒ and pass through a kissing-gate to the right of Fishponds Farmhouse to head for Ecclesbourne Glen.

The path descends into woodland and swings left and then right before coming to a footpath junction. Keep ahead to Ecclesbourne Glen and Hastings and keep right when the path divides to pass above the reservoir with its ranks of caravans on the far side. Keep ahead at Bollard 5, where a path goes right to Barley Lane and another runs off to the left. The path descends to the bottom of the glen and then becomes broad and grassy as it climbs to a crossways. Keep ahead to reach Barley Lane. Turn left for 80 yds (73m) and then fork left on to Rocklands Lane. Pass the entrance to Rocklands Holiday Park and keep on to East Hill. Skirt the edge of the pitch-and-putt course. *(If you wish to explore Hastings, follow the signs to Old Town; the funicular provides an effortless means of returning to the route at the start of the clifftop section.)*

The Old Town lies beneath the cliff, its narrow streets lined by all sorts of interesting shops, pubs, and restaurants, many offering locally caught fish. Fishing boats are drawn up on the beach, and some of the tall, weatherboarded net stores can still be seen. In contrast, westwards along the shore Regency buildings face the sea, arranged in crescents behind the promenade. The pier is well preserved and provides a good perspective of the coastline between Eastbourne and Dungeness.

If you are not descending to Hastings, make for the terminus of the funicular railway ⓓ and head east towards Fairlight Glen.

The return along the clifftop starts with a bracing walk on springy turf. Keep to the cliff-edge path and descend the steep steps to the mouth of Ecclesbourne Glen. The climb on the other side is taxing so a pause to look back at East Hill will be welcome.

Walk along the path, following the signs for Fairlight Glen. A storm in 2001 destroyed access to the secluded beach here. Look out for the signs of Fairlight church and Fire Hills and ahead on the clifftop you can see the outline of a radar installation by the former coastguard cottages. Climb more steps, turn right at the top and follow the cliff path beside a seat in memory of 'Sue'. Go through a kissing-gate and pass alongside the radar station. Return to the car park and visitor centre. ●

The Temple of the Winds from Fernhurst

		GPS waypoints	
Start	Fernhurst		SU 896 284
Distance	6 miles (9.7km)	**A**	SU 901 296
Approximate time	3 hours	**B**	SU 906 305
Parking	Car park off Vann Road in the centre of Fernhurst	**C**	SU 906 313
		D	SU 912 304
Refreshments	The Red Lion at Fernhurst	**E**	SU 918 301
Ordnance Survey maps	Landrangers 186 (Aldershot & Guildford) and 197 (Chichester & The South Downs), Explorer 133 (Haslemere & Petersfield)	**F**	SU 920 303
		G	SU 915 290
		H	SU 906 286

The Temple of the Winds was a summerhouse built at the summit of Blackdown by Alfred, Lord Tennyson when he lived at nearby Aldworth House. The summerhouse has gone but the viewpoint remains. At 919ft (280m) it is the highest point in the county.

Cross the main road at Fernhurst (A286) into Church Road and turn left after the church to pass the Red Lion inn. The church was virtually rebuilt by Anthony Salvin, a local resident, in the 19th century. Follow the road and as it bends left towards the main road, take the path on the right. Keep to it as it skirts a field to reach a stile. Cross a tarmac drive and continue ahead in the next field. Make for a stile at the top and keep ahead in the next pasture. When you reach another tarmac drive, keep right, following the right of way sign. Beyond a house take the path on the right, over a stile **A**. The path descends to the bottom of the valley, and there are ponds to the right.

The climb, to the other side of the valley, is steep. Bear right at the top to climb a low bank and join a bridleway. Turn left onto the grassy track, pausing to look back at the fine view.

Farther on, avoid a bridleway sign and a path running down to a tarmac drive and continue on the path parallel to it. On reaching the drive, turn right and walk along to the road by a sign for Sheetlands. Turn left here but, after Wadesmarsh Farmhouse, leave the road to the right **B** to enter the National Trust's Valewood Park. The parkland provides lovely walking with the house and lake to the right and specimen trees ahead. The path joins the drive from the house. After 250 yds (229m) leave the drive to the right for a footpath that climbs steps to a kissing-gate. At the top of the field **C** turn right to go through a gate and walk below the trees to a gate that is above cattle sheds and leads into the woods.

The path goes up through trees to a kissing-gate and footpath sign. Head straight on across the field, keeping trees on the right. Join the Sussex Border Path, go forward to a gate into Chase Wood and on to a track made

gloomy by overhanging rhododendrons. At a fork bear right to follow the Sussex Border Path then keep left immediately in front of a wooden gate and head uphill. Continue to follow the Border Path across a cleared area where groups of tall pines survive and keep right at a junction with a track. Walk along to a bridleway crossways **D** to reach open ground, where the way, at last, becomes level.

This is Black Down. After about ½ mile (800m) the path descends to a junction **E**. Keep left, avoiding a path on the extreme left, pass a sunken path on the right and when you reach several pools, turn right onto a bridleway. Keep

right immediately onto another bridleway **F**.

Take the left fork and when the way divides, continue along the ridge. Keep right at the next waymarked fork, then left at the next fork where there is a sign for the Serpent Trail. This path leads to the memorial seat to Mabel, wife of Edward Hunter, who gave Black Down to the National Trust in 1944. This was the site of the summerhouse erected by Tennyson during the 24 years that he occupied Aldworth House, the home he built a mile (1.6km) or so to the north. Remarkably this was open country until 1958 when the National Trust began to plant conifers.

Walk clockwise around the summit to pass a strategically placed rustic seat, pausing to enjoy the beautiful view, and then bear left on to a path that descends the spur to the south-west, between high banks. Turn right when it reaches a lane, but after a few yards **G** go left down a bridleway track which soon swings right. After a house, keep ahead at a bridleway junction on a path that leads down into woodland and that has at least a trickle of water flowing down most of the year. This is a refreshing part of the walk if you are wearing trainers. Cross a track and continue down the mossy-banked path, which merges with a waymarked track farther down. Keep ahead and at the point where it reaches a lane, at Tanyard Cottage **H**, turn right on to a path into woodland, with the stream to the right. This is a lovely finale to the walk. Bear right to walk with a field, and then Fernhurst's cricket ground, to the left. The path conveniently emerges into the village next to the Red Lion inn. Retrace your steps to the A286. ●

A stunning view from the site of The Temple of the Winds

Woolbeding Common and Hammer Wood

		GPS waypoints	
Start	Car park just before end of public road to Woolbeding Common	✐	SU 869 260
Distance	7 miles (11.3km)	Ⓐ	SU 864 261
Approximate time	4 hours	Ⓑ	SU 860 258
		Ⓒ	SU 850 256
Parking	At start (N.B. The car park is to the east of the lane)	Ⓓ	SU 838 250
		Ⓔ	SU 830 247
Refreshments	None	Ⓕ	SU 842 240
Ordnance Survey maps	Landranger 197 (Chichester & The South Downs), Explorer 133 (Haslemere & Petersfield)	Ⓖ	SU 855 234
		Ⓗ	SU 856 240
		Ⓙ	SU 862 247

Woolbeding is a tiny village close to Midhurst, with a church where services are held by candlelight. Its sandy common, owned by the National Trust, is on high ground to the north of the village. Below it lies extensive woodland, remnants of the Wealden oak forests. The walk blends airy heath with shady forest and passes a large hammer pond, a reminder that the district was once an important centre of the iron industry. Note the precipitous slope between Ⓔ and Ⓕ, which may be dangerous when wet.

✐ From the car park, turn right along the lane, pausing to admire the view to the west and north that takes in much of three counties. After 250 yds (229m) turn left off the road where a footpath crosses by a seat. Do not take the path that descends steeply from here but turn right to follow the ridge for 100 yds (91m) past a triangulation pillar hidden in the bushes just off the path. Now turn left onto the waymarked Serpent Trail and drop down to a bench seat and three-way fingerpost. Turn right, and contour along the foot of the ridge to a crossways at Barnett's Cottage.

Ⓐ Bear left past the house, to pass a second house on your left. Cross its drive, and descend with a fence on your left to cross another drive at Honeysuckle Cottage; now the waymarked path makes its way down through holly and oak woods to Linch Road. Take the footpath opposite that goes through woods before coming to a level, marshy area where there is a crossways. Keep ahead to come to a junction Ⓑ, where the path leaves National Trust land. Bear right (but do not follow the wall to the right) and then turn left at a T-junction. The path climbs gently through bracken to reach a driveway at Titty Hill.

Turn left and, where the surfaced road begins, fork left into the woods again. Leave the woods by a stile and follow a track behind the houses at Queen's Corner. Bear left by a garage to resume on a footpath at the entrance to

The view before **F**

Brandon Beeches. Cross the bottom of the field here to a T-junction. Turn left, then turn right over the stile at the edge of the woods **C** to walk westwards, with a fine view to the right.

Bear right at the end of the woods, and follow a churchyard wall to the stile on Milland Road (note that the church has been demolished). Cross the road to a second stile, then go across a pasture to a plank bridge and the stile leading into Kingsham Wood.

Keep the fence on your left, and follow the faint path past a signpost near a large beech tree. The way drops down to join a woodland track, and a stile takes the right of way out of the woods and into a field. Bear right to cross it to reach a stile in the corner **D** and turn right on to a track. This leads past Old Farm and onto its drive, which takes you to a road junction.

Take the road signposted to Borden Wood – Jungle Wood is to the right with its inappropriate pine trees. After ¼ mile (400m), where the road begins to climb more steeply, turn left onto a footpath and climb away from the road for 180 yds (165m).

E Leave the Serpent Trail here, and turn left onto a footpath that climbs

steeply (but briefly) after branching right from the main track. Bear left on to Green Lane and then right for a few yards along a road. Take the footpath on the left keeping close to the fence on the left, to come to a stile in the corner of the field. The path then descends a short but steep slope, veers to the right, and takes the left-hand fork along a ledge. The trail falls gently and then rises again, all the while clinging precariously to a precipitous slope. The final stretch is down a steep slope that would need great care in the wet. Turn right on to the sunken track at the bottom **F** to reach a lane.

Walk for a few yards along the lane before turning left into the woods belonging to Chithurst Forest Monastery. This section makes particularly pleasant walking, and the sweet chestnuts would be a bonus in autumn. There are glimpses of Hammer Pond as the path dips down to its southern end (there will probably be muddy patches here). Turn

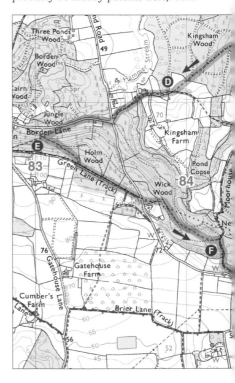

left when the path reaches Hammer Lane. On a hot day the shady coolness of the sunken byway is welcome. Cross Iping Lane onto the lane to Hammerwood, another ancient, sunken lane. Cross the stream at the bottom and then turn left **G** to climb into the wood. A mossy wall is soon close to the left and there is a beautiful long meadow beyond it. At the entrance to Ash House take the drive to the right and, just before reaching a house where the track swings left, look to the right to see a narrow sunken path **H** climbing into the wood.

This path takes you to a bridleway that passes a pond and then climbs steadily to a T-junction **J**. Go left and keep ahead when the surfaced road ends. Bear right when the track divides after Woolhouse Farm and then, at a complicated four-way junction, take the path that goes half-right into the woods. Cross the road to re-enter Woolbeding Common. The path climbs steadily to the lane but, instead of joining it at this point, it is more enjoyable to use one of the paths that wind across the heathland, roughly parallel to the lane, to return to the car park. ●

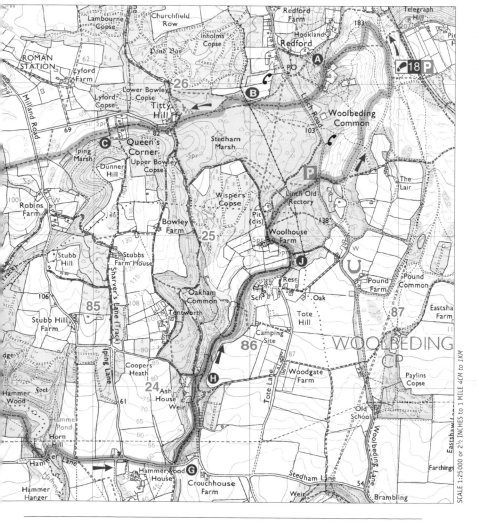

Beachy Head and Long Down

Start	Old Lighthouse, 1½ miles (2.4km) west of Beachy Head
Distance	6½ miles (10.5km)
Approximate time	3 hours
Parking	At start
Refreshments	The Beachy Head pub and adjoining café
Ordnance Survey maps	Landranger 199 (Eastbourne & Hastings), Explorer 123 (Eastbourne & Beachy Head)

GPS waypoints

- TV 566 954
- Ⓐ TV 556 960
- Ⓑ TV 564 957
- Ⓒ TV 563 962
- Ⓓ TV 593 969
- Ⓔ TV 597 969
- Ⓕ TV 590 956

After an initial appetiser of clifftop walking around the Old Lighthouse towards Birling Gap, the outward route is on a little-used bridleway that strikes eastwards across Long Down. A famous section of the South Downs Way provides the return, with stunning views of Beachy Head and the Seven Sisters as a climax. Parts of the route may be muddy.

From the car park below the Old Lighthouse, turn westwards and follow the grassy path to the right of the tarmac drive and climb to the lighthouse. Belle Tout was built in the 1830s but its light was often obscured by fog and low cloud. A new lighthouse replaced it in 1902. Belle Tout had a starring role in the popular television adaptation of Fay Weldon's novel *The Life and Loves of a She-Devil*. It was moved back from the edge of the cliff in 1999.

The view back towards the modern lighthouse, beneath Beachy Head, is spectacular. Walk to the other side of the lighthouse and the vista in the opposite direction, over the Seven Sisters to Birling Gap and Seaford, is also stunning.

The path descends westwards towards Birling Gap. When the pub at Birling Gap comes into view, take the grassy

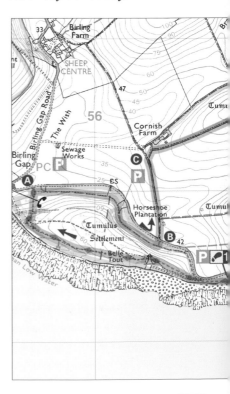

path to the right, which almost reaches the road. Bear right to leave the Lookout (a National Trust property) and join a bridleway heading eastwards, parallel to the road **A**. Keep to the right-hand path of the two parallel routes. There is a brief, pleasant spell of woodland walking through Horseshoe Plantation before the path drops down to the road. Cross it to the concrete track to Cornish Farm **B**.

Ignore a permissive bridleway to the right and continue on the track almost to the farm, turning off through a wooden bridlegate placed by an iron gate **C**. Go through a wooden gate by a

paddock and keep fencing on the right as you climb to the crest of Long Down. Pass through several gates and avoid a track on the right to Bullockdown Farm. Keep ahead between fences and stone walls before reaching a gate leading out to the road. Cross it and go forward on a grassy path with the buildings of Eastbourne seen ahead. When you reach a waymark, turn right and follow the Weald Way. Make for the next waymark and turn sharp left towards the seafront **D**. The path descends to give a fine view of the town. At the next seafront sign, turn sharp right to follow the South Downs Way **E**.

The path skirts the top of Whitebread Hole, which must once have been a

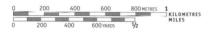

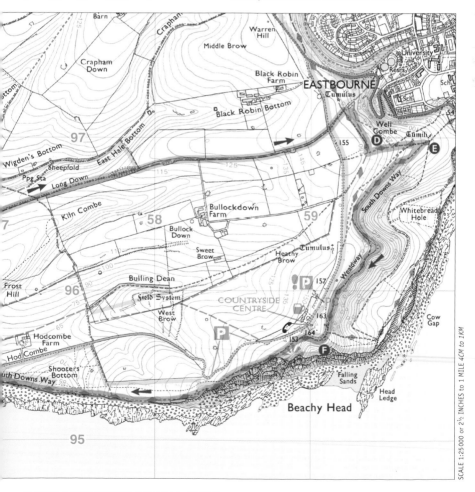

Beachy Head at dusk

spectacular landslip. Keep bearing to the left around the rim of the Hole, coming close to the road and then swinging away from it. Unfortunately, the path, occupying a narrow ledge, is becoming badly eroded, a process not helped by illegal horseriding. The situation is remedied as it approaches Beachy Head **F** where it is asphalted. This is necessary because of the crowds who come here by coach and car, few venturing far along the coast path.

The Countryside Centre has interactive displays illustrating the history of this part of the South Downs and how man and beast have been influenced by the unstable geology.

Refreshments are available close by.

The lighthouse, 536ft (163m) below the clifftop, is best seen from near the parking area about ¼ mile (400m) past the pub, where the road makes a hairpin turn. On a clear day the view extends 40 miles (64km) to the east to Dungeness, while in the opposite direction you may see the outline of the Isle of Wight, 80 miles (130km) away.

For the rest of the way, walking is a delight on springy turf away from all the crowds. There is an energetic switchback at the conclusion, with the cliffs at their most spectacular, before the path comes close to the road at the starting point. ●

Downland Hills from Devil's Dyke

		GPS waypoints	
Start	Devil's Dyke inn	🖉	TQ 258 110
Distance	8 miles (12.9km)	Ⓐ	TQ 252 107
Approximate time	3½ hours	Ⓑ	TQ 223 105
Parking	At start	Ⓒ	TQ 240 074
Refreshments	Devil's Dyke Inn; hot drinks and	Ⓓ	TQ 239 080
	ices at Mile Oak Farm Shop	Ⓔ	TQ 249 091
Ordnance Survey maps	Landranger 198 (Brighton &	Ⓕ	TQ 247 101
	Lewes), Explorer 122 (Brighton & Hove)		

A fine walk along the escarpment of the South Downs, from Devil's Dyke to Truleigh Hill, is followed by a long, gentle descent towards Brighton with views towards the sea. The return is on paths and bridleways with equally undemanding gradients. Be sure to choose a day with good visibility.

If the wind is blowing strongly enough from the sea, paragliders and hang-gliders provide colourful entertainment at the start of this walk. The Devil's Dyke is a natural feature of the landscape, a dry valley adapted as a defensive enclosure in the Iron Age. The Victorians constructed a funicular railway to the summit from Poynings, and there was also a cable-car across the valley. Both ceased to operate many years ago.

🖉 Walk back along the road for a few yards and then bear right across the grass to climb a stile and head towards a derelict building. The triangulation pillar is to the left. The views are

Paragliders above Devil's Dyke

magnificent and open up seaward as you swing westwards towards the radio masts at Truleigh Hill. The path reaches a gate at the entrance to the National Trust's Fulking Escarpment.

A Although complex on the map, this junction is straightforward on the ground. Fork gently right after the gate and join the South Downs Way, a bridleway that follows the crest of the downs westwards. Fulking village can be seen below as a foreground to the vast panorama to the north. The track dips to pass below power lines and then climbs Edburton Hill. Keep to the South Downs Way and pass the radio masts on Truleigh Hill. About ¼ mile (400m) farther on, just past Truleigh Hill Farm **B**, turn left on to a bridleway and walk past Freshcombe Lodge, heading towards the sea.

If paragliders are flying they will just be visible in the far distance, close to the Devil's Dyke pub, 2½ miles (4km) away. The Monarch's Way, a long-distance path commemorating King Charles II's flight into exile, joins from the right before Thundersbarrow Hill. The National Trust owns the land at Southwick Hill, a little farther on. Keep ahead as the track gradually descends towards the suburbs of Brighton. When the track leaves National Trust land it goes above the tunnel carrying the A27. Continue for 250 yds (229m) until you reach a wooden gate on the left.

C Turn left through the gate and follow the hedge on your right for a few paces, then turn sharp left onto a track that joins the Sussex Border Path. The track drops downhill beneath power lines and recrosses the tunnel, then continues to a T-junction marked by metal gates and a stile.

D Turn right for 60 yds (55m). *If you wish, keep straight on here for 200 yds (183m) for hot drinks and ice creams at Mile Oak Farm Shop.* To continue the

walk, swing hard left through the wooden gate to begin the steady climb up Cockroost Hill. After 325 yds (297m) the track goes through another gate at a footpath junction. Bear left and carry

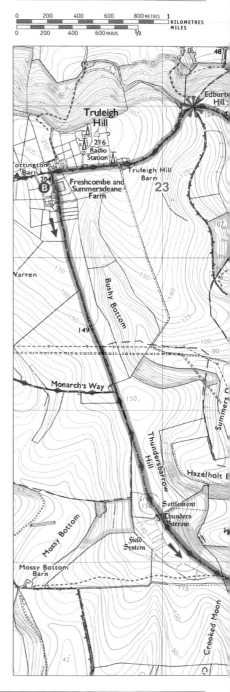

on up the hill, passing Mile Oak Dew Pond on your left. At length the track swings to the right and continues to a T-junction.

E Turn left and continue the steady climb back towards the downland ridge. This long straight section ends at a gate that takes you back into the National

Trust's estate.

F Fork hard right after the gate onto the waymarked bridleway, a lovely grassy trail that rejoins your outward route at point **A**. From here, simply retrace your steps for the final short section back to the starting point at the Devil's Dyke Inn. ●

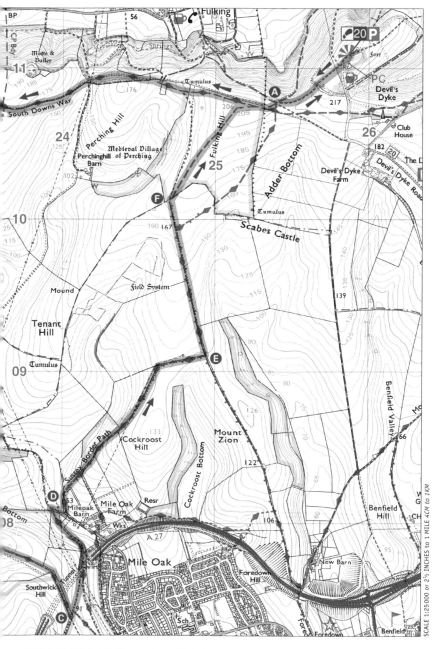

Lodsworth and Lickfold from Cowdray Park

Lodsworth and Lickfold from Cowdray Park

		GPS waypoints	
Start	Benbow Pond, Cowdray Park		
Distance	8 miles (12.9km)	🖉	SU 914 222
Approximate time	4 hours	**Ⓐ**	SU 918 229
		Ⓑ	SU 918 238
Parking	At start	**Ⓒ**	SU 918 248
Refreshments	The Hollist Arms, Lodsworth	**Ⓓ**	SU 931 254
		Ⓔ	SU 940 258
Ordnance Survey maps	Landranger 197	**Ⓕ**	SU 942 248
	(Chichester & The South Downs),	**Ⓖ**	SU 930 232
	Explorer 133	**Ⓗ**	SU 928 227
	(Haslemere & Petersfield)	**Ⓙ**	SU 924 224

This typically Wealden walk covers a wide tract of woods and fields to the north-east of Midhurst. Lodsworth is a byway village typical of the area – although fortunately, unlike many, it still has its pub.

🖉 Walk up the slope at the end of the pond and go through the kissing-gate at the top into a large meadow. Keep the fence to the right and follow it to a stile at the end of a line of trees. Cross the stile, bear left along the edge of the field, then swing right to follow an old hedgeline as far as a stile at the top of Heathend Copse.

Ⓐ Cross the stile and turn left onto a bridleway that divides almost immediately. Fork left up the charming sunken way, which will be muddy in wet weather. Continue climbing past the turning to Loves Farm until the track comes into the open just before Vining Farm, giving a lovely view to the south. Keep straight on at the crossways and carry on past the farmhouse, continuing to climb towards a pylon ahead. There is a crossways by the pylon Ⓑ. Keep ahead to descend past the pylon, heading towards a mast on top of a wooded ridge. Bear right at the entrance to a grassy field and descend to begin more than a mile (1.6km) of woodland walking.

Keep ahead at the crossways at the foot of Hoe Hill and climb the steep slope. Keep ahead into Snapelands Copse where a bridleway joins from the right. Pass the cottage at Ovis Common, which enjoys a fine view eastwards. The bridleway divides after Rose Cottage – turn off the drive to the right Ⓒ and descend a little-used bridleway, which often has wet patches.

The track drops to a young conifer plantation, and a bridleway branches off to the left; about 200 yds (183m) farther on, turn sharp right at the way-mark post. After joining a drive by a cottage, you soon reach a road. Turn left and, 50 yds (46m) after Collyers Cottages, go right on to a field path that passes through two paddocks and reaches the left-hand corner of woodland, where there is a plank bridge and a stile. Turn right on a field-edge path that skirts a wood to reach another stile and bridge

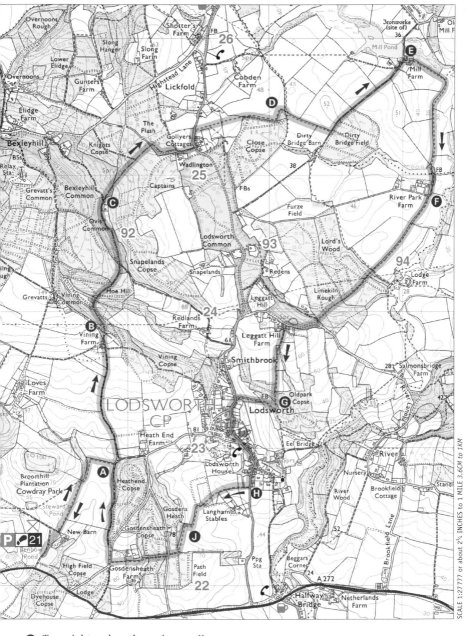

D. Turn right and go through a small gate before turning left to walk towards the woodland at Dirty Bridge Field.

Turn left at the woodland on to a broad track. Go past the farmhouse at Mill Farm and then take the footpath on the right through the farmyard **E**. Keep the hedge to the left as far as a signposted stile; cross over, and turn right to continue by the hedge but now on the other side. At the end of lengthy meadows, go through a metal gate on to a track and pass to the left of a large pond. Continue until the track swings right. Turn off it to the left here **F** over a stile and walk with the hedge to the right towards pylons.

A rural scene near Lodsworth

A stile leading into Lord's Wood ends this section of field-walking. Tall bracken is an obstacle as the path goes below the power lines and then crosses a track before continuing through the woods and crossing another track. The way becomes narrow as it begins to climb more steeply, and brambles snatch at your clothing. At the top, turn left to reach a road and then right to continue the climb to Leggatt Hill Farm.

Pass through its white gates and keep ahead through a wooden field gate on a track that twists right and then left to a metal gate. Go through this and walk with the hedge to the right through a long meadow. A stile and metal gate lead the path into Oldpark Copse. Keep ahead here, and descend to a footpath junction amidst the conifers.

G Turn sharp right onto a better path that soon reaches a plank bridge and climbs to a road. Turn left to walk through Lodsworth, passing the Hollist Arms at its centre. Continue down the hill and keep to the main street as it leaves the village past Woodmancote, the house where E H Shepard spent the last years of his life.

H Just beyond the last house, turn right onto the field path that climbs through two paddocks and runs diagonally across the corner of the next field. From here, follow the waymarked route through a gap in the hedge, and turn right along the field edge to a fingerpost at the corner of the field.

J Turn left and follow the woodland edge until you reach the second set of electricity wires at the corner of the field. Turn right here, cross the stile by an electricity post, and follow the wires down to a lane.

After 140 yds (128m) turn left onto the signposted bridleway, just after Gosdens Heath. The track immediately splits into three; take the narrow middle way through the bracken and follow it into the woods where it opens out and climbs steadily back to **A**. Turn left to retrace your steps to the starting point at Benbow Pond. ●

Kingley Vale, Stoughton and Walderton

Kingley Vale, Stoughton and Walderton

		GPS waypoints	
Start	Car park at West Stoke	🖉	SU 824 088
Distance	8½ miles (13.7km)	Ⓐ	SU 823 099
Approximate time	4½ hours	Ⓑ	SU 825 113
Parking	The car park is on the west side of the village, on the lane to Funtington	Ⓒ	SU 824 121
		Ⓓ	SU 796 115
		Ⓔ	SU 792 107
Refreshments	Pubs at Stoughton and Walderton	Ⓕ	SU 800 103
Ordnance Survey maps	Landranger 197 (Chichester & The South Downs), Explorer 120 (Chichester)	Ⓖ	SU 823 098

A pleasant 20-minute stroll takes you to the small museum at Kingley Vale National Nature Reserve. From here, the walk follows a waymarked nature trail through sinister yet fascinating glades of yew trees, which may be the oldest living things in this country. The path climbs to the summit of Bow Hill before crossing woodland and downland to the attractive villages of Stoughton and Walderton, each of which has a pub. The return is through similar countryside, with lovely views from the crest of the downs.

🖉 From the car park, take the surfaced footpath to Kingley Vale, which passes through open country at first and then woodland before the vale comes into view, a vast bowl of trees rising to the crest of the downs. The entrance to the nature reserve is ahead, where a bridleway skirts the lower edge of the vale.

Ⓐ Go through the kissing-gate and spend a few minutes looking around the interesting little field museum. The reserve covers 150 acres (61 ha) and includes the largest surviving yew forest in the world. Legend has it that the yew forest has grown from trees planted over the graves of soldiers slain in battle in 895, when a Viking army

was put to flight by Saxons. The downland turf supports nearly 50 species of flowering plants, and 12 types of orchid grow in moist areas. No fewer than 39 species of butterfly have the area as their habitat, and at the top of the vale there are 14 prehistoric monuments.

Now follow the waymarked nature trail on the main path into the woodland, which is a mixture of oaks and yews. The latter have grown convoluted over the centuries and, in the gloom, they make the place sinister. It is a relief to emerge into the clearing at nature trail point 11, and follow the grassy path to the far side of the bowl. Your way lies due north, striking up the steep hillside straight ahead along an eroded chalky path that soon re-enters the trees just inside the woodland edge. When you finally reach the grassy expanse at the top pause to recover breath and take in the wonderful view over Chichester Harbour to the Isle of Wight. Keep ahead for 50 yds (46m) before turning right to see the Tansley Stone, the monument to Sir Arthur Tansley, who founded the reserve in 1957.

Turn back across the grassy area and, without descending, go over a stile to a group of Bronze Age tumuli known as the Devil's Humps. Even wider views are seen from here.

Take the track eastwards that passes close to the tumuli – part of the Western Downs Cycle Route. The track meanders through an ash grove below the summit of Bow Hill before reaching a bridleway crossways.

B Turn left past an information panel, climbing at first but then dropping down more steeply. Pass a bridleway junction and a row of giant Leylandii interspersed with yews until the woods fall away to the left and Stoughton comes into view in the distance. Join the track that merges from the left here, and continue to the bridleway crossways 125 yds (114m) farther on.

C Turn left onto the Monarch's Way long-distance path, which follows the edge of a wood – there is a seat to the right at the end of the wood. Follow the chalky track that descends to Stoughton, pass the isolated farm buildings, then bear right through the farmyard at Old Bartons and turn left onto the road. Pass, or pause at, the Hare and Hounds before reaching the village green. Fork right here onto the bridleway, leaving the telephone box on your left and St Mary's Church to the right. The bridleway climbs steadily on the edge of a wood.

Pass a bridleway sign and fork left

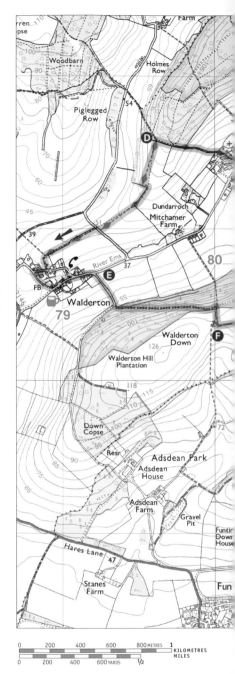

where the track divides but at the next one **D**, where the bridleway swings right, turn left to follow a footpath across a field, heading for the upper end of a line of trees. Then walk ahead with trees to the right before crossing

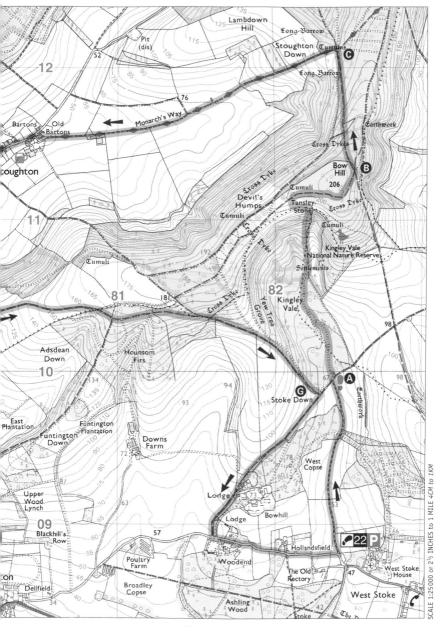

another large field to the end of the hedgerow and trees opposite. Cross a lane and continue in the same direction, following the hedge. The path goes by the gardens of new bungalows to reach a lane. Turn right and then take the footpath on the left when the lane swings right to cross a stream and reach Walderton's main street. Turn left past

the Barley Mow inn and walk eastwards through the village until you reach the last house on the right.

E Now turn right up the unmarked gravel track that climbs gently between hedgerow trees to the edge of the woods on Walderton Down. Fork left here onto the 'Bridle Road to Kingley Vale' and climb steadily through beech trees. Fork right at a clearing near the top to reach the crest of Walderton Down by a ruined barn.

G Turn left here and follow the enclosed bridleway, climbing all the time and enjoying the wonderful views to the south. Keep straight ahead along the waymarked bridleway when you reach Hounsom Firs, where the track at last levels off. After 120 yds (110m) bear left when another bridleway leaves to the right; then bear right to remain on the bridleway when it divides opposite open ground to the left. The path

A cottage at Walderton

descends past yew trees, and another bridleway leaves to the left. Keep ahead, descending gently on a path that gives magnificent views southwards and has grassy spots where you may rest to enjoy them. See if you can spot the spire of Chichester Cathedral as the path swings to the right after joining the gravel track coming down the flank of Kingley Vale.

The gentle descent ends at a T-junction **G**. Turn right on to the enclosed bridleway that soon reaches the edge of a wood. Turn right at a T-junction by Bowhill House and then turn left at the lane to return to West Stoke. ●

Blackcap and Stanmer Down from Ditchling Beacon

Blackcap and Stanmer Down from Ditchling Beacon

		GPS waypoints	
Start	Ditchling Beacon	📍 TQ 333 129	
Distance	8½ miles (13.7km)	Ⓐ TQ 370 125	
Approximate time	4 hours	Ⓑ TQ 384 118	
Parking	At start	Ⓒ TQ 376 112	
Refreshments	None en route	Ⓓ TQ 363 110	
Ordnance Survey maps	Landranger 198 (Brighton & Lewes), Explorer 122 (Brighton & Hove)	Ⓔ TQ 350 098	
		Ⓕ TQ 347 108	

At 813ft (248m) the Ditchling Beacon is the third-highest summit on the South Downs. The beacon gave warning of the coming of the Armada in 1588. The route follows the South Downs Way at first – a National Bridleway Trail that is popular with cyclists. The Way turns off southwards near Blackcap, and the walking is then through comparatively deserted countryside. Note that there are few waymarks on Balmer Down so careful map-reading is essential.

The land around the Beacon was given to the National Trust to serve as a monument to a young pilot shot down in the Second World War.

📍 Cross the road from the car park and head eastwards along the South Downs Way, passing a dew pond on the right. The view to the north is an early highlight of the walk. At first the going is excellent on springy turf over Western Brow, keeping on the crest of the hill. A bridleway joins at the top of Streat Hill and, after crossing a lane, the surface underfoot becomes flinty on a rough track. The village of Plumpton lies below with its sprawling agricultural college.

After walking for nearly an hour you will enter the National Trust's Blackcap property. Here the South Downs Way

leaves to the right Ⓐ. About 100 yds (91m) past this junction, bear right when the track divides, leaving the triangulation pillar to the left. A lonely post marks a bridleway crossways – keep to the main track going ahead to come to a gate by an electricity pylon. Go through the gate and, after 80 yds (73m), turn right Ⓑ by a National Trust sign on to a bridleway leading through woodland.

Continue for 250 yds (229m), then turn right through a gate and follow the waymarked bridleway diagonally across a field. Prominent posts in the fence ahead indicate the position of the next gate, and the waymarked route continues towards a clearing in the scrub on the far hillside. After another

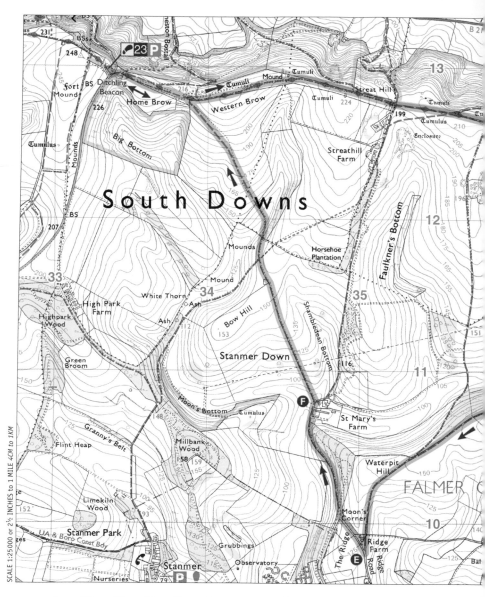

SCALE 1:25000 or 2½ INCHES to 1 MILE 4CM to 1KM

gate the bridleway follows the hedge down to an opening. Turn right and descend to a crossways at the bottom of the valley **C**.

Cross a track to a gate and from here climb to the former gateway near the top of a tree-topped knoll. This will prove to be a false summit as the path continues to climb after the wooded area. Keep ahead along the field edge to come to a set of gates at a complicated junction. From here, the right of way swings in an arc close to a line of scrubby bushes to reach a waymarked wooden gate.

D Go through the gate, cross the track and the neck of the field beyond it, then turn left onto a grassy track by the fence that leads past a small wood. After this there is a lovely view to the right over St Mary's Farm; a bridleway joins from the right, and the track bears left to descend Waterpit Hill. Soon the derelict buildings of Ridge Farm herald

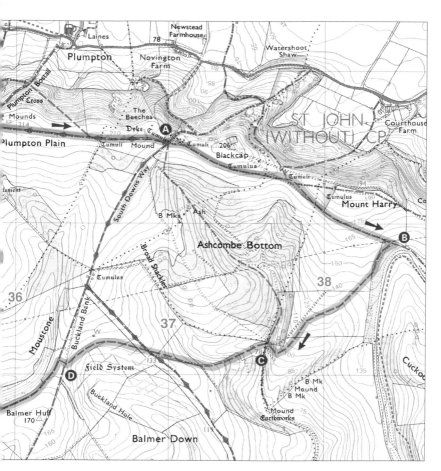

the junction with Ridge Road about ½ mile (800m) to the north of Falmer (the University of Sussex falls within the parish).

Turn right **E** away from the village and climb the lane, looking back to see the university buildings as you pass a large wood.

F Fork left through a waymarked gate at St Mary's Farm. The track crests the flank of Stanmer Down and continues through a gate along the left-hand field edge. A gate in the left-hand hedge marks a crossways, before the path drops through a wooden gate into a small sequestered valley.

A further gate opens onto the path that climbs steadily over the left-hand flank of

Western Brow; at the summit, a small wooden gate returns you to the South Downs Way. Turn left and retrace your outward steps to the Beacon. ●

The view from Ditchling Beacon

Burwash and Bateman's

		GPS waypoints	
Start	Burwash village centre		
Distance	7½ miles (12.1km)	🖉 TQ 672 246	
Approximate time	3 hours	Ⓐ TQ 671 238	
		Ⓑ TQ 657 226	
Parking	Free car park at start	Ⓒ TQ 653 213	
Refreshments	Burwash offers The Bear and The	Ⓓ TQ 665 214	
	Bell pubs and Lime Tree tearoom.	Ⓔ TQ 664 221	
	There is a tearoom at Bateman's	Ⓕ TQ 669 233	
Ordnance Survey maps	Landranger 199 (Eastbourne & Hastings), Explorers 136 (The Weald, Royal Tunbridge Wells) and 124 (Hastings & Bexhill)		

Starting in the straggling village of Burwash, this delightful walk heads south into the undulating landscape of the Dudwell Valley. Woodland provides ample shade on a warm day though in one or two places the path can get a little overgrown at the height of summer – but only briefly. The return leg offers impressive views back towards Burwash.

🖉 Turn left out of the car park and follow the main road through Burwash. Pass the village hall, dated 1907, and eventually turn left at the National Trust sign for Bateman's. Drop down the hill; this road can get busy with traffic when the house is open to the public. On reaching Bateman's, keep right at the road junction Ⓐ.

This historic house was the home of the celebrated writer Rudyard Kipling between 1902 and his death in 1936. Built by a local ironmaster in 1634, Bateman's is now in the care of the National Trust and open to the public during the summer. 'We have loved it ever since our first sight of it,' Kipling once wrote. He was also a keen motorist and his vintage Rolls Royce is on display in the grounds.

Follow the bridleway alongside the grounds, cross a bridge over the River Dudwell and turn right by Corner Cottage. Skirt a pond and stay on the grassy path. Pass a seat and go through a wooden gate into woodland. Avoid a path on the right, running across a foot-

Bateman's at Burwash

bridge, and continue through the wood, following it beside a stream. Make for a kissing-gate and follow the obvious path across the meadow to a galvanised gate. Cross a bridge over a ditch

immediately beyond it and turn right along a field boundary. In the corner go through another gate into the next meadow. Ignore a waymarked footpath over on the right and keep ahead on the grassy path. Go uphill to a wood, cross several stiles among the trees and continue ahead across farmland,

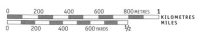

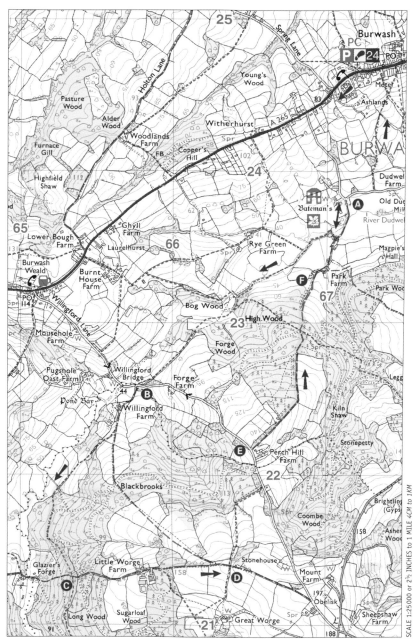

The Dudwell Valley

keeping hedgerow on the left. Cross a stile and keep ahead to another stile leading out to the lane **B**.

Cross over to a bridleway gate, pass between hedges and keep to the left of Willingford Farm. Beyond it make for the far right corner of the field and follow the signposted footpath. Take the path across several pastures and look for a gate leading into extensive woodland. Occasional waymarks guide you through the trees. Eventually you reach a bridleway **C**.

Turn left here, following the track to Little Worge Farm. Go through a gate and keep to the right of a thatched barn and the farmhouse. Continue on a concrete track and pass a bridleway running off sharp left. Turn left about 120 yds (110m) beyond it just before a cottage **D**.

Cross a stile and go through a gate. Keep over towards the right-hand side of the field and cross the next pasture, heading for the far right corner. Look for a stile by some trees, cross over and keep left along the perimeter of the next pasture. There are trees on the left. Make for an opening and exit to the

road. Turn left and walk along to Perch Hill Farm, branching right onto a track immediately beyond it **E**.

Keep ahead on a path when the track peters out at a stone cottage and follow it along the edge of woodland. This stretch of the walk can get a little overgrown in places during high summer. A path comes in from the left at the point where the main right of way broadens. On reaching a junction with a track in a clearing, turn left for several places, then right.

Continue on the bridleway, go through a galvanised gate and look for Bateman's and Park Farm some distance ahead across the fields. Pass through woodland, make for the farm out-buildings **F** and continue along the track.

On reaching Bateman's at **A** turn right and pass a giant oak tree. Keep ahead to a path and stile on the left, follow the field edge and then go diagonally across the next pasture towards the top boundary. Cross a stile, keep left in the field and make for two stiles and a footbridge in the corner. Keep left, following the fence, and after the next stile take the left-hand path at the immediate fork. Follow it back to the car park at Burwash. ●

Bosham and Fishbourne from West Itchenor

		GPS waypoints	
Start	West Itchenor		
Distance	9½ miles (15.3km)	🖉	SU 798 012
Approximate time	5 hours	Ⓐ	SU 807 008
Parking	At start	Ⓑ	SU 815 005
Refreshments	Pubs at Apuldram, Fishbourne,	Ⓒ	SU 826 010
	Bosham and West Itchenor	Ⓓ	SU 829 013
Ordnance Survey maps	Landranger 197 (Chichester &	Ⓔ	SU 839 039
	The South Downs),	Ⓕ	SU 837 045
	Explorer 120 (Chichester)	Ⓖ	SU 829 034
		Ⓗ	SU 801 031

This route is dependent on the ferry that crosses from Bosham to West Itchenor. It operates a daily service from mid-May until the end of September and at weekends and bank holidays from April until the end of October (Tel. 07970 378350). For times of tides call Chichester Harbour Conservancy on 01243 512301. It is best to avoid high tides. The end of the walk is a two-mile (3.2km) hike along the edge of the mudflats from Bosham Creek. Altogether this route makes a memorable day out.

🖉 From the car park, walk to the main street and turn left. After 50 yds (46m), opposite the Ship inn, take the footpath on the right to Itchenor Sailing Club and turn right on to the shoreline path. Make the most of the river views as they last for only ¼ mile (400m) or so before splendid houses oblige the path to divert inland. It is interesting however, to see these properties from the right of way: the road that ends at Westlands Copse by the entrance to Spinney and Mallard Creek. Head away from the river here Ⓐ, following the edge of the wood. Keep ahead at a footpath junction to join a concrete track at Westlands Farm.

The track becomes a lane. After 100 yds (91m) on this, turn left into Greenacres and follow the drive to the right Ⓑ before leaving it to the left at the next bend, by a cylindrical leylandii. There is another brief stretch along the shoreline before the path strikes inland along the edge of a field with woodland to the left. When it joins a lane, keep ahead past a junction to pass Birdham Shipyard. Keep ahead past Birdham Pool but leave the lane by keep-

West Itchenor

ing ahead at a crossways **C** on a path that turns left to cross the lock gates of Salterns Lock, the last lock of the Chichester Canal, an inland waterway that once linked London with Portsmouth. Walk by the side of the canal for 200 yds (183m) before turning left at the waymark to head for the marina office. Cross the lock gate here (you may have to wait at busy times), pass the toilets and then turn immediately left towards the harbour. Turn right after a few paces to enter a copse, keeping left at the immediate fork **D** to follow a permissive path through the copse and close to the shoreline with a distant view of Chichester Cathedral. Head inland around a property to reach a road and turn left to reach the Crown and Anchor pub at Dell Quay. Join the waterside path near the pub and follow it towards Fishbourne, keeping to the left of a stile. Cross a channel and stay on the path along the flood bank to savour the wide views of sky and

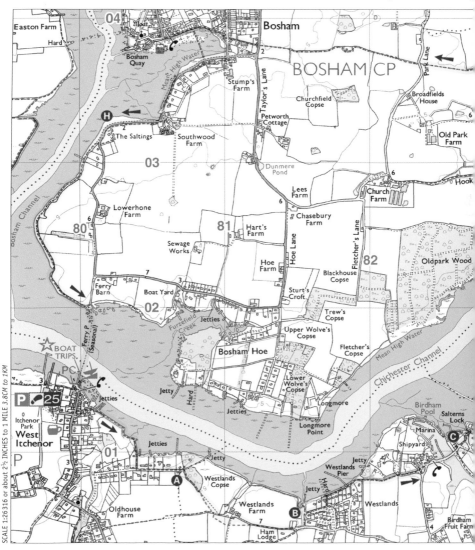

saltings even when a short-cut is offered to the right **E**.

Bear left after crossing a creek and cross a sparkling stream by footbridge and then a plank causeway over Fishbourne Meadows, which was part of the Roman harbour. *You can turn right at the end of the lane by the Mill* **F** *if you want refreshment at the Bull's*

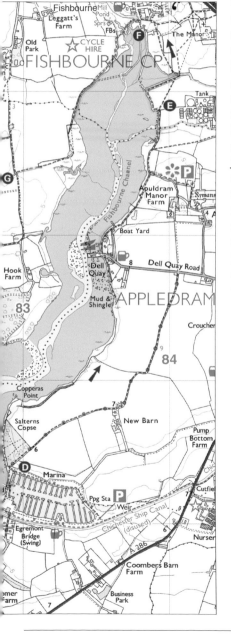

Head. Alternatively, keep ahead across the lane on to the footpath that leads into a reedbed. Footbridges keep feet above the tide, and the path soon climbs above the reeds on to the flood wall on the west side of the harbour.

There are more views of Chichester Cathedral over the mud flats as you walk southwards. The path goes through strange woodland of stunted oak trees and passes a pond before swinging west, away from the river. At a T-junction **G** turn right and then go left at the next junction. Pass alongside a line of trees and then cut between crops to reach Park Lane. Keep ahead on to an enclosed path, which is featureless but has the virtue of being straight. It swerves round an isolated cottage to join its drive. The right of way leaves the drive when the latter bends left and then crosses two bridges. Continue on a field path and cross a lane to a house named 'Byways'. Pass the house to join an enclosed path and reach the head of Bosham Creek. The pubs and other delights of the village are to the right, the route continues to the left.

Follow Shore Road around the south side of the creek. Note that if the tide is favourable you can take a short-cut across the mud on a causeway and stepping stones if you have visited the village. If the tide is high you may have to use the footpath to the left of the road.

After The Saltings the road swings away from the shore **H**. Keep ahead along the shoreline *(this is difficult when the tide is exceptionally high)*. The wonderful mix of sky and water, and the subdued colours of The Saltings make this a particularly beautiful part of the route – and there are so many seabirds and waders as well. Just when it seems that the ferry landing is completely mythical it comes into view, the causeway snaking over the mud. The trip across the river is a fitting end to the walk. ●

Cuckmere River and Norton Top from Alfriston

		GPS waypoints	
Start	Alfriston		
Distance	9 miles (14.5km)		TQ 521 032
Approximate time	4½ hours	**A**	TQ 519 015
		B	TQ 509 011
Parking	The Willows – the long-stay car park on the left of the main road on the northern approach to the town	**C**	TQ 488 023
		D	TQ 498 050
		E	TQ 506 058
		F	TQ 512 054
Refreshments	The Plough and Harrow at Litlington, the Rose Cottage Inn at Alciston. There are also pubs at Alfriston and Berwick	**G**	TQ 518 049
Ordnance Survey maps	Landranger 199 (Eastbourne & Hastings), Explorer 123 (Eastbourne & Beachy Head)		

A route that covers riverside and downland inevitably involves a climb or two, but the gradients on this route are reasonably easy and the views outstanding. Half-time refreshment can be taken in village pubs on the homeward leg.

If possible use the long-stay car park on the east side of the road as you enter Alfriston.

Take the footpath that runs down the town side of the coach park. Go over the stile and through a disused farmyard to reach the riverbank. Make for the distinctive white bridge just a few paces away. Cross to the east bank and turn right for Exceat, following the South Downs Way beside the course of the Cuckmere River. Look across the water to see the delicate tracery of the east window of Alfriston Church – often called the 'Cathedral of the Downs'. There are also glimpses of the town's other old buildings – the 14th-century Clergy House was built to cater for parish priests after the Black Death while the Star Inn dates from the 15th century and is part timbered.

Look to the left as well and you may see a heron lazily take to the wing from the dykes surrounding the water-meadows. Litlington is reached after 20 minutes or so. Keep to the riverbank path unless you would like to visit the Plough and Harrow inn or the village tearoom, both up a short footpath on the left. Otherwise, cross the footbridge to the west side of the river.

Follow the path southwards for about ¼ mile (400m) and, at the first stile, turn right **A** to climb towards the White Horse on Cradle Hill. Keep ahead at a post marking a footpath junction. A little farther on, where the track from Tile Barn joins, it becomes a bridleway that eventually reaches a gate giving on to a road. Do not go through the gate but turn left to follow the grassy path

0	200	400	600	800 METRES 1	
					KILOMETRES
					MILES
0	200	400	600 YARDS	½	

The view from above Bopeep Chalk Pit

below the road to a stile. Bear right at the top of the enclosed path to reach the High and Over car park on Cradle Hill.

Cross the road and turn right for 50 yds (46m) to find a stile **Ⓑ** on to the National Trust's Frog Firle land. The short footpath joins the bridleway (known as The Comp) that follows a downland ridge for more than four miles (6.4km) from this point.

After a gate where another bridleway joins, keep right and the way gradually swings to the north along the edge of a golf course. At the end of the latter there is a bench by a crossways **Ⓒ**, and now the views are unobstructed eastwards across Blackstone Bottom to the rolling countryside beyond. This is exhilarating walking – after Norton Top the way is level but above Bostal Bottom the land is cultivated and the bridleway joins a farm track.

This joins the road to the car park above Bopeep Chalk Pit, and the stunning view northwards is revealed here. As you descend the road you will find magnificent blackberries that are ripe for eating in late July. Where the road begins a hairpin bend to the left,

leave it for a footpath on the right **Ⓓ**, going through a gate and then turning left to follow the waymark to Alciston.

The path is shady through woodland but, when it emerges from the trees, climb the stile on the left and descend along the edge of a field, keeping trees to your right. Turn right at a track and then left into the village passing a beautiful flint Tithe Barn and walking past the drive to the church to reach the Rose Cottage inn **Ⓔ**.

Turn right opposite the pub, cross a stile and then turn right at the barn. Now make for the left-hand edge of the churchyard wall. Cross a stile and turn right, then almost immediately left. Follow the field edge to a T-junction, turn left and then right at a second T-junction **Ⓕ** to join a concrete track into Berwick. At yet another T-junction you can either turn left for a refreshment stop at the Cricketers Inn or go right to continue on the route past the south side of the church.

Turn right here **Ⓖ** to take a footpath heading southwards between fields. Keep ahead when it meets a lane and turn left through the short-stay car park to reach the car park on the other side of the main street.   ●

Downland Walk from Telscombe

		GPS waypoints	
Start	Telscombe, 4 miles (6.4km) south of Lewes	🖍	TQ 404 032
Distance	11 miles (17.7km)	Ⓐ	TQ 399 032
Approximate time	5 hours	Ⓑ	TQ 383 052
		Ⓒ	TQ 378 050
Parking	On the broad verge beyond the youth hostel at south end of village	Ⓓ	TQ 378 058
		Ⓔ	TQ 367 073
Refreshments	None	Ⓕ	TQ 379 079
Ordnance Survey maps	Landranger 198 (Brighton & Lewes), Explorer 122 (Brighton & Hove)	Ⓖ	TQ 391 067
		Ⓗ	TQ 413 049

Although it is only four miles (6.4km) from Lewes, little Telscombe feels like the most remote of all downland villages. You are more likely to meet horse-riders than other walkers on the first part of the route, which leads ever deeper into the heart of the downs and mainly stays on the ridge. When it descends, the wayside wild flowers are a wonderful recompense.

🖍 The road runs up to a gate and cattle-grid. Take the bridleway to the right, a track leading towards a pair of houses. The sea is to the left and the downs extend in every other direction. Turn right Ⓐ before reaching the drives to the two houses on to a bridleway that heads north, by a fence. It joins a track opposite a modern installation to the left. Keep ahead where a footpath goes to the right and a bridleway leaves to the left. There is a good view to the left over Saltdean before you pass a derelict shed on the right where a barn is now visible in the fields to the left. This is Sussex downland at its best, and in spring and summer hosts of butterflies rise from the wayside flowers, even though the fields are cropped. There is a prominent monument by the path where John Harvey died suddenly on June 20,

1819. He was a notable country gentleman from Bedfordshire and had probably come to Brighton believing that the new resort would be good for his health.

Pass the memorial and soon you reach the next junction Ⓑ. Bear left to descend towards a cattle-shed. Climb a slope to a gate and turn right Ⓒ on a bridleway, which is part of a South Downs Circular Walk (but a different one to this).

The track heads into a deserted landscape with all habitation soon lost to sight. At a large stand of sycamore and ash trees, turn right Ⓓ to head for roofless cattle-sheds. Keep ahead at the bridleway junction by the sheds to pass below a clump of trees and go through a gate, now walking on a grassy path on the right-hand side of a dry valley. The wild flowers are spectacular and skylarks sing above.

At the top of Falmer Bottom the bridleway goes through a gate by a National Nature Reserve sign and ahead on a track. This passes through part of Castle Hill National Nature Reserve, where the steep slopes have never been cultivated by machinery and have a wide variety of chalk-loving plants, many of them rare. The one steep climb of the walk comes with the ascent of Newmarket Hill, up the coomb from Falmer Bottom. Go through the gate at the top and turn right **E** to join Jugg's Road (an ancient track that runs directly to Lewes) and the South Downs Way. This stretch of grassy walking is a highlight of the route, with the sea in the distance to the right and a vast expanse of downland revealed on the left beyond the A27 and the railway. The modern pattern of vast fields is only relieved by a few smaller ones.

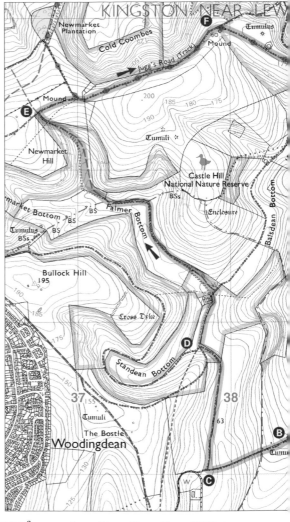

On reaching a stile and galvanised gate on Jugg's Road, go straight on for Lewes or branch right **F** to follow the South Downs Way. Continue for some time, meet Dencher Road joining from the left and 200 yds (183m) farther on a gate takes the path to the other side of the fence. After a bridleway (coming from near the Harvey monument) joins at the crest, turn left **G** on to a concrete road that makes rather monotonous walking for almost two miles (3.2km). At least you have a view of the Seven Sisters in the distance ahead and the

going is easy.

Keep ahead when the concrete track meets another one to follow a bridleway along the field edge. Cross White Way and climb Mill Hill and then cross a drive going to a house to stay with the South Downs Way. At the bottom, turn right to leave the long-distance path **H** and walk through the farmyard. The track winds up through Cricketing Bottom before bending left at a waymark, then swinging right to climb steeply to the lane leading to Telscombe. Keep right and return to the village. ●

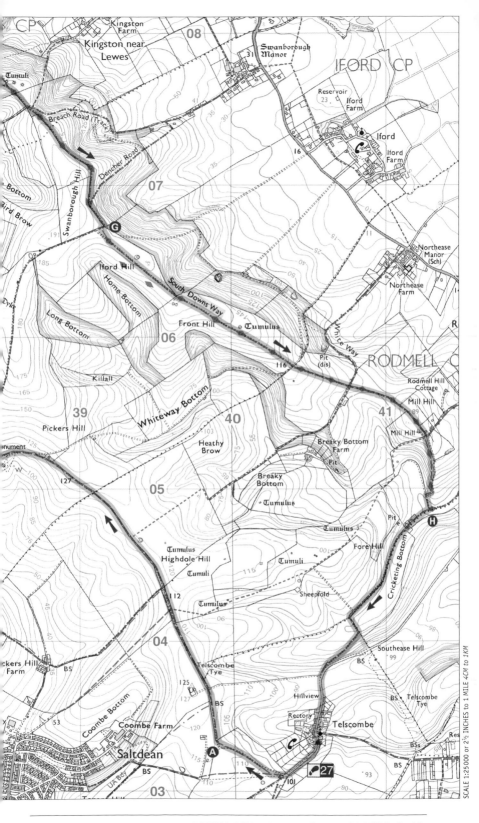

SCALE 1:25000 or 2½ INCHES to 1 MILE 4CM to 1KM

Bignor Hill and the River Arun

		GPS waypoints
Start	Summit of Bignor Hill	
Distance	Option 1: 11 miles (17.7km)	🖉 SU 973 129
	Option 2: 8½ miles (13.5km).	Ⓐ SU 989 132
	Option 3: 5 miles (8km)	Ⓑ TQ 000 119
Approximate time	Option 1: 5 hours. Option 2: 4½	Ⓒ TQ 024 118
	hours Option 3: 2½ hours	Ⓓ TQ 025 099
Parking	At start	Ⓔ TQ 018 113
		Ⓕ TQ 000 111
Refreshments	Riverside pub, brasserie and	Ⓖ SU 996 112
	tearooms at Houghton Bridge;	Ⓗ SU 988 113
	pub in Houghton village	
Ordnance Survey maps	Landranger 197 (Chichester & The South Downs),	
	Explorer 121 (Arundel & Pulborough)	

This varied and flexible route offers something for everyone. All the walks include woodland trails and an invigorating stretch of the South Downs Way. Options 1 and 2 both feature attractive sections beside the River Arun, while the longest route also passes the delightful little church at South Stoke. There are no refreshment stops on Option 3.

The surfaced road to Bignor Hill ends at the parking area, where the signpost underlines the significance of the hill to the Romans by pointing in the direction of Londinium and Noviomagus (Chichester).

🖉 Turn back down the road towards Londinium but fork right away from the road and climb the flinty track to the summit of Bignor Hill on the South Downs Way. There are wonderful views as the track leaves National Trust land.

Keep on the South Downs Way as it descends and swings left to come to a crossways below Westburton Hill.

Ⓐ Bear right past the cattle shed to follow the South Downs Way as it climbs steadily along the side of Westburton Hill towards woodland. About a mile (1.6km) further on, the path divides at a copse on the right.

Ⓑ *Turn right to follow Option 3 heading due south along the edge of Langham Wood to rejoin the longer route at Ⓕ.*

Otherwise, keep straight on along the main track as the A29 comes into view ahead. Turn right onto the main road and, after about 80 yds (73m), cross it to a continuation of the South Downs Way – a track that descends steeply with Coombe Wood to the left. At the end of the wood the river comes into view with Bury church to the left, one of the most memorable of Downland panoramas.

Cross the road at the bottom and follow the South Downs Way to cross the graceful new bridge. Turn right along the north bank of the River Arun and stay on the riverbank path when the South Downs Way leaves to the left. The path skirts a residential caravan site before reaching a road at Amberley. Turn right to pass the Bridge Inn and the Boathouse Brasserie and head out onto Houghton Bridge

C *To follow Option 2, cross the bridge and turn immediately left over the stile onto the riverside footpath; this section may be boggy in wet weather. After ¹⁄₂ mile (800m) turn right to rejoin the longer route at* **E**.

Just halfway across the bridge, the main route turns left onto an islet and follows the southern riverbank for 650 yds (594m) before coming to a footbridge across a dyke. After this it turns left, away from the river, and is narrow and somewhat overgrown with brambles and roses. Turn right when you reach Stoke Road and follow the lane to a T-junction at North Stoke. Go left at the telephone box and then immediately right on to a field path that at first heads directly towards the slender spire of the church at South Stoke. Cross a delightful little suspension

bridge into woodland, where the shade is welcome on a hot day. The path at length emerges on to the lovely riverbank near the bridge at South Stoke. Cross the bridge and climb past St Leonard's Church with its spire, which would seem more at home on a bank of the Rhine than the Arun.

Take the bridleway to the right from the lane immediately after South Stoke Farm **D**, where the stables are in the same style as the church. Pass the back of this building and then turn left on to a bridleway above the river. There is a steep climb along the edge of a field with a fine view at the top.

The path is well above the river for much of the way to Houghton with Arundel Park wall to the left. A kissing-gate brings another footpath to join the riverside path (this is the Monarch's Way, named to celebrate Charles II's flight through Sussex to exile in France). Beware of exposed tree roots where the path is squeezed between wall and river. The river is invariably muddy, and it would be dangerous to

Cyclists on the South Downs Way

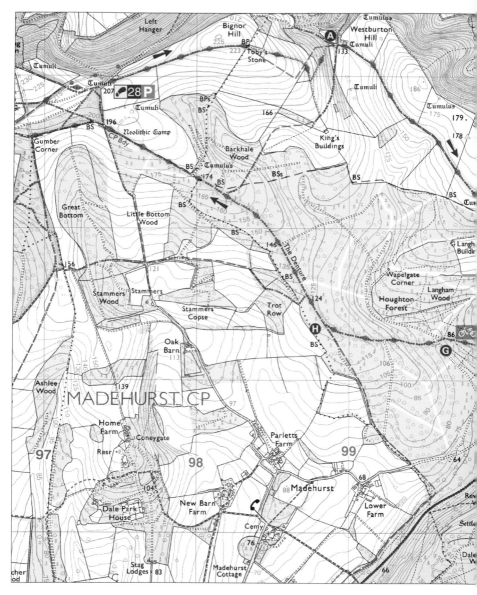

swim in it. There is a clearing with a chalky cliff face above, which is a popular place for a barbecue.

E *Option 2 rejoins the main walk here.*

When the path meets a lane, climb it to the main road and turn left to pass the George and Dragon, where King Charles is said to have stopped for a pint or two. Take the private road that branches to the right just beyond the

pub but, after 20 yds (18m), follow the 'walkers' sign on to a bridleway between the drive and the road. This climbs steadily and crosses another drive before becoming a field-edge path giving fine views to the left over the valley. The gradient eases, and the path becomes enclosed and passes close to a car park. At the end of a long section of woodland walking you emerge to cross a field to the A29.

Cross the main road to continue on the bridleway ahead (now waymarked

towards the South Downs Way). When it swings to the right and starts to climb steeply, leave it to the left **F**.

Option 3 rejoins the main walk here.

Walk down a short length of well-used track to reach a broad cycleway. Turn right on to this right of way, which descends gently.

G Fork left 50 yds (46m) after the 'Please respect other users' notice, and then cross another track.

Now the path begins to climb more seriously. When it levels out another bridleway joins from the left **H**, and there is pleasant walking on a broad, grassy, straight track that climbs gently past yet another bridleway on the left. Now settle into your stride for a mile (1.6km) of steady climbing. The view opens up on the right as you pass a National Trust sign, and the gradient finally eases at a crossways with a wide vista on your left. Turn right here, keeping the woods on your left, to climb the final 300 yds (274m) to the car park.

●

Further Information

The National Trust

Anyone who likes visiting places of natural beauty and/or historic interest has cause to be grateful to the National Trust. Without it, many such places would probably have vanished by now.

It was in response to the pressures on the countryside posed by the relentless march of Victorian industrialisation that the trust was set up in 1895. Its founders, inspired by the common goals of protecting and conserving Britain's national heritage and widening public access to it, were Sir Robert Hunter, Octavia Hill and Canon Rawnsley: respectively a solicitor, a social reformer and a clergyman. The latter was particularly influential. As a canon of Carlisle Cathedral and vicar of Crosthwaite (near Keswick), he was concerned about threats to the Lake District and had already been active in protecting footpaths and promoting public access to open country-side. After the flooding of Thirlmere in 1879 to create a large reservoir, he became increasingly convinced that the only effective way to guarantee protection was outright ownership of land.

The purpose of the National Trust is to preserve areas of natural beauty and sites of historic interest by acquisition, holding them in trust for the nation and making them available for public access and enjoyment. Some of its properties have been acquired through purchase, but many of the Trust's properties have been donated. Nowadays it is not only one of the biggest landowners in the country, but also one of the most active conservation charities, protecting 581,113 acres (253,176 ha) of land, including 555 miles (892km) of coastline, and over 300 historic properties in England, Wales and Northern Ireland. (There is a separate National Trust for Scotland, which was set up in 1931.)

Furthermore, once a piece of land has come under National Trust ownership, it is difficult for its status to be altered. As a result of parliamentary legislation in 1907, the Trust was given the right to declare its property inalienable, so ensuring that in any subsequent dispute it can appeal directly to parliament.

As it works towards its dual aims of conserving areas of attractive countryside and encouraging greater public access (not easy to reconcile in this age of mass tourism), the Trust provides an excellent service for walkers by creating new concessionary paths and waymarked trails, maintaining stiles and foot bridges and combating the ever-increasing problem of footpath erosion.

For details of membership, contact the National Trust at the address on page 94.

The Ramblers' Association

No organisation works more actively to protect and extend the rights and interests of walkers in the countryside than the Ramblers' Association. Its aims are clear: to foster a greater knowledge, love and care of the countryside; to assist in the protection and enhancement of public rights of way and areas of natural beauty; to work for greater public access to the countryside; and to encourage more people to take up rambling as a healthy, recreational leisure activity.

It was founded in 1935 when, following the setting up of a National Council of Ramblers' Federations in 1931, a number of federations earlier formed in London, Manchester, the Midlands and elsewhere came together to create a more effective pressure group, to deal with such problems as the disappearance and obstruction of footpaths, the prevention of access to open mountain and moorland and increasing hostility from landowners. This was the era of the mass trespasses, when there were sometimes violent confrontations between ramblers and gamekeepers, especially on the moorlands of the

Hastings

Peak District.

Since then the Ramblers' Association has played an influential role in preserving and developing the national footpath network, supporting the creation of national parks and encouraging the designation and waymarking of long-distance routes.

Our freedom to walk in the countryside is precarious and requires constant vigilance. As well as the perennial problems of footpaths being illegally obstructed, disappearing through lack of use or extinguished by housing or road construction, new dangers can spring up at any time.

It is to meet such problems and dangers that the Ramblers' Association exists and represents the interests of all walkers. The address to write to for information on the Ramblers' Association and how to become a member is given on page 94.

 Walkers and the Law

The *Countryside and Rights of Way Act 2000 (CRoW)* extends the rights of access previously enjoyed by walkers in England and Wales. Implementation of these rights began on 19 September 2004. The Act amends existing legislation and for the first time provides access on foot to certain types of land – defined as mountain, moor, heath, down and registered common land.

Where You Can Go
Rights of Way
Prior to the introduction of *CRoW* walkers could only legally access the countryside along public rights of way. These are either 'footpaths' (for walkers only) or 'bridleways' (for walkers, riders on horseback and pedal cyclists). A third category called 'Byways open to all traffic' (BOATs), is used by motorised vehicles as well as those using non-mechanised transport. Mainly they are green lanes, farm and estate roads, although occasionally they will be found crossing mountainous area.

Rights of way are marked on Ordnance Survey maps. Look for the green broken lines on the Explorer maps, or the red dashed lines on Landranger maps.

The term 'right of way' means exactly what it says. It gives a right of passage over what, for the most part, is private land. Under pre-CRoW legislation walkers were required to keep to the line of the right of way and not stray onto land on either side. If you did inadvertently wander off the right of way, either because of faulty map reading or because the route was not clearly indicated on the ground, you were technically trespassing.

Local authorities have a legal obligation to ensure that rights of way are kept clear and free of obstruction, and are signposted where they leave metalled roads. The duty of local authorities to install signposts extends to the placing of signs along a path or way, but only where the authority considers it necessary to have a signpost or waymark to assist persons unfamiliar with the locality.

The New Access Rights
Access Land
As well as being able to walk on existing rights of way, under the new legislation you now have access to large areas of open land. You can of course continue to use rights of way footpaths to cross this land, but the main difference is that you can

Further Information

now law-fully leave the path and wander at will, but only in areas designated as access land.

Where to Walk

Areas now covered by the new access rights – Access Land – are shown on Ordnance Survey Explorer maps bearing the access land symbol on the front cover.

'Access Land' is shown on Ordnance Survey maps by a light yellow tint surrounded by a pale orange border. New orange coloured 'i' symbols on the maps will show the location of permanent access information boards installed by the access authorities.

Restrictions

The right to walk on access land may lawfully be restricted by landowners. Landowners can, for any reason, restrict access for up to 28 days in any year. They cannot however close the land:

- on bank holidays;
- for more than four Saturdays and Sundays in a year;
- on any Saturday from 1 June to 11 August; or
- on any Sunday from 1 June to the end of September.

They have to provide local authorities with five working days' notice before the date of closure unless the land involved is an area of less than five hectares or the closure is for less than four hours. In these cases landowners only need to provide two hours' notice.

Whatever restrictions are put into place on access land they have no effect on existing rights of way, and you can continue to walk on them.

Dogs

Dogs can be taken on access land, but must be kept on leads of two metres or less between 1 March and 31 July, and at all times where they are near livestock. In addition landowners may impose a ban on all dogs from fields where lambing takes place for up to six weeks in any year. Dogs may be banned from moorland used for grouse shooting and breeding for up to five years.

In the main, walkers following the routes in this book will continue to follow existing rights of way, but a knowledge and understanding of the law as it affects walkers, plus the ability to distinguish access land marked on the maps, will enable anyone who wishes to depart from paths that cross access land either to take a shortcut, to enjoy a view or to explore.

General Obstructions

Obstructions can sometimes cause a problem on a walk and the most common of these is where the path across a field has been ploughed over. It is legal for a farmer to plough up a path provided that it is restored within two weeks. This does not always happen and you are faced with the dilemma of following the line of the path, even if this means treading on crops, or walking round the edge of the field. Although the later course of action seems the most sensible, it does mean that you would be trespassing.

Other obstructions can vary from overhanging vegetation to wire fences across the path, locked gates or even a cattle feeder on the path.

Use common sense. If you can get round the obstruction without causing damage, do so. Otherwise only remove as much of the obstruction as is necessary to secure passage.

If the right of way is blocked and cannot be followed, there is a long-standing view that in such circumstances there is a right to deviate, but this cannot wholly be relied on. Although it is accepted in law that highways (and that includes rights of way) are for the public service, and if the usual track is impassable, it is for the general good that people should be entitled to pass into another line. However, this should not be taken as indicating a right to deviate whenever a way becomes impassable. If in doubt, retreat.

Report obstructions to the local authority and/or the Ramblers' Association.

Countryside Access Charter

Your rights of way are:

- public footpaths – on foot only. Sometimes waymarked in yellow
- bridle-ways – on foot, horseback and pedal cycle. Sometimes waymarked in blue
- byways (usually old roads), most 'roads used as public paths' and, of course, public roads – all traffic has the right of way

Use maps, signs and waymarks to check rights of way. Ordnance Survey Explorer and Landranger maps show most public rights of way

On rights of way you can:

- take a pram, pushchair or wheelchair if practicable
- take a dog (on a lead or under close control)
- take a short route round an illegal obstruction or remove it sufficiently to get past

You have a right to go for recreation to:

- public parks and open spaces – on foot
- most commons near older towns and cities – on foot and sometimes on horseback
- private land where the owner has a formal agreement with the local authority

In addition you can use the following by local or established custom or consent, but ask for advice if you are unsure:

- many areas of open country, such as moorland, fell and coastal areas, especially those in the care of the National Trust, and some commons
- some woods and forests, especially those owned by the Forestry Commission
- country parks and picnic sites
- most beaches
- canal towpaths
- some private paths and tracks Consent sometimes extends to horse-riding and cycling

For your information:

- county councils and London boroughs maintain and record rights of way, and register commons
- obstructions, dangerous animals, harassment and misleading signs on rights of way are illegal and you should report them to the county council
- paths across fields can be ploughed, but must normally be reinstated within two weeks
- landowners can require you to leave land to which you have no right of access
- motor vehicles are normally permitted only on roads, byways and some 'roads used as public paths'

 ## Global Positioning System (GPS)

What is GPS?

GPS is a worldwide radio navigation system that uses a network of 24 satellites and receivers, usually hand-held, to calculate positions. By measuring the time it takes a signal to reach the receiver, the distance from the satellite can be estimated. Repeat this with several satellites and the receiver can then use triangulation to establish the position of the receiver.

How to use GPS with Ordnance Survey mapping

Each of the walks in this book includes GPS co-ordinate data that reflects the walk

position points on Ordnance Survey maps.

GPS and OS maps use different models for the earth and co-ordinate systems, so when you are trying to relate your GPS position to features on the map the two will differ slightly. This is especially the case with height, as the model that relates the GPS global co-ordinate system to height above sea level is very poor.

When using GPS with OS mapping, some distortion – up to 16ft (5m) – will always be present. Moreover, individual features on maps may have been surveyed only to an accuracy of 23ft (7m) (for 1:25000 scale maps), while other features, e.g. boulders, are usually only shown schematically.

In practice, this should not cause undue

Further Information

difficulty, as you will be near enough to your objective to be able to spot it.

How to use the GPS data in this book

There are various ways you can use the GPS data in this book.

1. Follow the route description while checking your position on your receiver when you are approaching a position point.

2. You can also use the positioning information on your receiver to verify where you are on the map.

3. Alternatively, you can use some of the proprietary software that is available. At the simple end there is inexpensive software, which lets you input the walk positions (waypoints), download them to the gps unit and then use them to assist your navigation on the walks.

At the upper end of the market Ordnance Survey maps are available in electronic form. Most come with software that enables you to enter your walking route onto the map, download it to your gps unit and use it, alongside the route description, to follow the route.

Walking Safety

Although the reasonably gentle countryside that is the subject of this book offers no real dangers to walkers at any time of the year, it is still advisable to take sensible precautions and follow certain well-tried guidelines.

Always take with you both warm and waterproof clothing and sufficient food and drink. Wear suitable footwear, such as strong walking boots or shoes that give a good grip over stony ground, on slippery slopes and in muddy conditions. Try to obtain a local weather forecast and bear it in mind before you start. Do not be afraid to abandon your proposed route and return to your starting point in the event of a sudden and unexpected deterioration in the weather.

All the walks described in this book will be safe to do, given due care and respect, even during the winter. Indeed, a crisp, fine winter day often provides perfect walking conditions, with firm ground underfoot and a clarity unique to this time of the year. The most difficult hazard likely to be encountered is mud, especially when walking along woodland and field paths, farm tracks and bridleways – the latter in particular can often get churned up by cyclists and horses. In summer, an additional difficulty may be narrow and overgrown paths, particularly along the edges of cultivated fields. Neither should constitute a major problem provided that the appropriate footwear is worn.

Useful Organisations

Campaign to Protect Rural England
128 Southwark Street, London SE1 0SW
Tel. 020 7981 2800
www.cpre.org.uk

East Sussex County Council
County Hall, St Anne's Crescent,
Lewes, East Sussex BN7 1UE
Tel. 01273 481000
www.eastsussex.gov.uk

Forestry Commission
Silvan House, 231 Corstorphine Road,
Edinburgh EH12 7AT
Tel. 0131 334 0303
www.forestry.gov.uk

Forest Enterprise – South East England Forest District
Bucks Horn Oak, Farnham,
Surrey GU10 4LS
Tel. 01420 23666
www.forestry.gov.uk

Long Distance Walkers' Association
www.ldwa.org.uk

National Trust
Membership and general enquiries:
PO Box 39, Warrington WA5 7WD
Tel. 0870 458 4000

South East
Polesden Lacey, Dorking, Surrey RH5 6BD
Tel. 01372 453401
www.nationaltrust.org.uk

Natural England
Northminster House,
Peterborough PE1 1UA
Tel. 0845 600 3078
www.naturalengland.org.uk

Ordnance Survey
Romsey Road, Maybush,
Southampton SO16 4GU
Tel. 08456 05 05 05 (Lo-call)
www.ordnancesurvey.co.uk

Ramblers' Association
2nd Floor, Camelford House,
87–90 Albert Embankment,
London SE1 7TW
Tel. 020 7339 8500
www.ramblers.org.uk

Society of Sussex Downsmen
10 The Drive, Hove, East Sussex BN3 3JA
Tel. 01273 771906

South Downs Campaign
P.O. Box 3473, Brighton BN1 7FZ
Tel. 01273 563358
www.southdownscampaign.org.uk

Tourist information:
www.visitsoutheastengland.com

Local tourist information offices:
Arundel: 01903 882268
Battle: 01424 773721
Bexhill-on-Sea: 01424 732208
Bognor Regis: 01243 823140
Brighton & Hove: 0906 711 2255 (50p/min)
Chichester: 01243 775888
Eastbourne: 01323 411400
Hastings: 01424 781111
Horsham: 01403 211661
Lewes: 01273 483448
Littlehampton: 01903 713480
Midhurst: 01730 817322/815933
Rye: 01797 226696
Seaford: 01323 897426
Worthing: 01903 210022

Youth Hostels Association
Trevelyan House, Dimple Road,
Matlock, Derbyshire DE4 3YH
Tel. 01629 592600
www.yha.org.uk

West Sussex County Council
County Hall, West Street,
Chichester, West Sussex PO19 1RQ
Tel. 01243 777100
www.westsussex.gov.uk

 Ordnance Survey maps of Sussex

The area of Sussex is covered by Ordnance Survey 1:50 000 (1¼ inches to 1 mile or 2cm to 1km) scale Landranger map sheets 196, 197, 198 and 199. These all-purpose maps are packed with information to help you explore the area. Viewpoints, picnic sites, places of interest and caravan and camping sites are shown, as well as public rights of way information such as footpaths and bridleways.

To examine the area in more detail and especially if you are planning walks, Ordnance Survey Explorer maps at 1:25 000 (2½ inches to 1 mile or 4cm to 1km) scale are ideal:

120 Chichester
121 Arundel & Pulborough
122 Brighton & Hove
123 Eastbourne & Beachy Head
124 Hastings & Bexhill
125 Romney Marsh, Rye & Winchelsea
133 Haslemere & Petersfield
134 Crawley & Horsham
135 Ashdown Forest
136 The Weald, Royal Tunbridge Wells

To get to the Sussex area use the OS Travel Map-Route Great Britain at 1:625 000 (1 inch to 10 miles or 4cm to 25km) scale or OS Travel Map-Road 8 (South East England including London) at 1:250 000 (1 inch to 4 miles or 1cm to 2.5km) scale.

Ordnance Survey maps and guides are available from most booksellers, stationers and newsagents.

www.totalwalking.co.uk

www.totalwalking.co.uk
is the official website of the Pathfinder®
and Short Walks guides. This interactive
website features a wealth of information
for walkers – from the latest news on route
diversions and advice from professional
walkers to product news, free sample
walks and promotional offers.